SING WILLOW

SING WILLOW

Jeremy Paul

Illustrated by Tim Jaques

The Book Guild Ltd
Sussex, England

First published in Great Britain in 2002 by
The Book Guild Ltd
25 High Street,
Lewes, East Sussex
BN7 2LU

Typesetting in Times by
Keyboard Services, Luton, Bedfordshire

Printed in Great Britain by
Bookcraft (Bath) Ltd, Avon

A catalogue record for this book is available from
The British Library

ISBN 1 85776 688 1

To my wife Pat, and my daughters Amanda, Tara, Sasha and Sophie – what a team!

In affectionate memory of Tom Tatham.

CONTENTS

Foreword ix

Acknowledgements xi

Openers 1

1   The Squirearchy 7

2   The Survival of the Fittest 31

3   Dad's Army 63

4   'Pritch' 87

5   Ewen 121

6   Family Matters 136

7   'Pandora's Box' 144

8   'It'll All Be the Same': 'The Invalid Centenary
      Match' 154

Closure: 'Good God, Said God...' 169

FOREWORD

I have to confess I was predisposed to love this book before I'd read a page of it. Jeremy it was who killed me so elegantly in *Upstairs Downstairs*; the suicide note he wrote for my dismal *alter ego* Major James Bellamy was beautiful and for months I enjoyed the rare treat of people telling me in the street how glad they were to see me 'alive'. Since then he has remained a close friend and one whose work I always enjoy greatly. SING WILLOW is a delightful book, lovingly compiled, about the history and fortunes of the Invalids, a cricket club whose purpose perfectly evokes the ethos of A.G. Macdonell's *England Their England*. The team itself does for local cricket what *The Full Monty* does for hen parties. Jeremy's book reminds me so much of all that I am homesick for when I have to be abroad during an English summer; village greens, prep school humour, the sound of rain on chestnut trees, warm local beer, scones to die for, the smell of linseed oil etc... In short the cricket season. It seems that to be involved with the Invalids is to be in a blissful rose-tinted time-warp. As President of the Nettlebed and Swyncombe Cricket Club I always look forward eagerly to our fixture against the Invalids, it gives us a chance to try out some new blood without any being spilled. It combines a perfect opportunity for showbiz gossip with a very fine approximation of cricket: best of all it gives me a chance to catch up with JP. Happily, as his time at the crease seems to diminish each year, we have longer to chat.

SING WILLOW is packed with intriguing information, some truly heroic tales of derring-do at the crease and lots of very funny drawings and anecdotes. Nobody who loves the game of cricket, or even just loves someone who loves the game of cricket, should be without a copy to read during that bleak time called the football season.

Simon Williams,
May, 2002.

ACKNOWLEDGEMENTS

The author and publishers wish to thank the following for their kind permission to reproduce extracts in this book: *Evening Standard* (Londoner's Diary, 1969); Faber & Faber for *The Faber Book of Cricket*; Hutchinson for *Most Generous of Men* by Patrick Howarth; Picador for *England Their England* by A G Macdonnell; *The Times* (Roger Gray obituary, 1992). The extract from *Against Travel Writing* by Robyn Davidson, published in *Journeys* by Picador (and first published in *Granta 72*), is reprinted by permission of PFD on behalf of Robyn Davidson.

Special thanks for their contributions to:

Tom Tatham, Bill Foss, Edward Bishop, Norman Neale, David Pritchett, Ewen Gilmour, Betty Boyd and Nina Clarke, Richard Butler, John Timbers, Jeremy Kemp, John Divett, Mike Halliwell, Bill Rodwell, Paul Southon, Simon Collins, John Shepherd, Kevin Moore, Clive Seigal, David Money, Geoffrey Hartley, John Stanley, Mike Seabrook, Gerald Howat, Dudley Carew, Godfrey Smith, Eric Warburg, James Lipscombe, The Cricketer International and many, many more...

Not to mention all our village opponents over the years without whom...

And special thanks to David Atkins.

OPENERS

Don't forget Saturday morning Charing Cross Underground Station (ran the telegram) 10.15 sharp whatever you do don't be late Hodge.

So begins the classic account of the village cricket match in A.G. Macdonell's *England Their England*. His inspiration was Sir John Squire's incomparable Invalids. The game was played on a hot summer day in the 1920s in the fictional Kentish village of Fordenden. It was scheduled to start at 11.30. The charabanc hired to carry the team left Charing Cross at 12.30, two players short, to travel the 50 miles into cricket folklore.

At 2.30, after halts at Catford, the White Hart at Sevenoaks, the Angel at Tunbridge Wells, and three smaller inns at tiny villages, the charabanc drew up triumphantly beside the cricket ground. At twenty minutes to 3, Mr Hodge had completed his rather tricky negotiations with the Fordenden captain, and had arranged that two substitutes should be lent by Fordenden in order that the visitors should field eleven men, and that nine men on each side should bat. But just as the two men on the Fordenden side, who had been detailed for the unpleasant duty of fielding for both sides and batting for neither, had gone off home in high dudgeon, a motor car arrived containing not only Mr Hodge's two defaulters but a third gentlemen in flannels as well, who swore stoutly that he had been invited by Mr Hodge to play and affirmed that he was jolly well going to play. Whoever stood down, it wasn't going to be him. Negotiations therefore had to be reopened, the pair of local Achilles had to be recalled, and at ten minutes to 3 the match began upon a twelve-a-side basis.

On 7 May 2000, the Invalids brought a team to play the real village of Crondall led by Mr Paul (your guide through these pages). In the Plume and Feathers he discovered to his embarrassment that 14 players were gathered with one yet to arrive. He knew he'd selected 12 and was prepared himself to stand down. One of the extras, Mr Mathews, he dimly remembered asking at the pre-season drinks party on Mr Halliwell's floating bistro, but he'd had been unable to confirm because Mr Mathews had been on holiday in France. Blessed with a sweet and forgiving nature, Mr Mathews accepted there was no place for him, but he came to watch, kit at the ready, and brought with him the team's revered but also unselected wicket-keeper, Mr Southon, as a drinking companion. It was the presence of the 15th player, Mr Kent from Australia, which floored the skipper. Mr Kent swore stoutly that he'd been invited by Mr Paul in the pre-season drinks party and affirmed he was jolly well going to play. Mr Paul recalled the moment now and also that he had failed to record it. Things began to sort themselves out when Crondall announced they had no wicket-keeper. After four pints and a (jolly super) Sunday roast, Mr Southon was plucked out of the pub and at ten minutes to 3 the match began upon a twelve-a-side basis.

It should be noted that Mr Southon performed for the village with distracted efficiency, and the visitors' own wicket-keeper, Dr Cantor, arrived at twenty minutes past 3, having mistaken the A3 for the M3.

At the end of an absorbing game (a tight draw), everyone

returned to the Plume professing themselves well satisfied. Add to the 15 players, the magisterial presence of Mr Jupe, the umpire, and a back-up team including three players' wives and at least five of their offspring, we can be assured that the flame of the Invalids burns bright as ever in the new millennium, and not much has changed since that vividly 'historic day in Fordenden', 75 odd years ago.

But much ale has flowed under the bridge. Scores of diverse and fascinating characters have been called to the famous colours, some of them, by chance or persuasion, no mean cricketers. And it's a remarkable fact, probably unique in wandering club cricket that the Invalids have had only four Captains in their 80-year history: Sir John Squire, Alastair Boyd, David Pritchett and Ewen Gilmour – four individuals of strongly differing character and temperament who have left their mark on proceedings, while at the same time allowing the club to flow blissfully on unimpeded.

England has survived a Second World War and changed out of all recognition. Cricket itself has changed, but something with the Invalids seems to have stuck and held fast. Quite how and why this has happened is hard to fathom, but these pages, with the aid of some wonderfully precise and fallible memories, will attempt to fill in just a few of the gaps.

It all began with ...

SIR JOHN SQUIRE

Born in Devon on April Fool's Day in 1884, John Collings Squire was one of the central figures of the English literary world in the 1920s and 30s. Educated at Blundell's and St John's College, Cambridge, he was the first literary editor of the *New Statesman* but his major achievement was the creation of the *London Mercury* magazine, which encouraged and published the flowering talent of English lyric poetry after the First World War. He also founded the Architecture Club; saved Stonehenge and Carlton House Terrace from spoliation; and was the first man to give a radio commentary on the Boat Race. He stood twice for Parliament, first as a Labour candidate, then as a Liberal. His friends were puzzled by the switch, since Labour was on the upswing at the time and the Liberals were sinking fast. But he gave his reason that he would have stood for anything to get the incumbent Chiswick representative out. On this latter occasion, a tense recount ensued, not to decide the winner but to determine whether Squire lost his deposit. He did, both times, and chucked his political ambitions.

In 1932, 500 people sat down to dinner at the Dorchester to celebrate Jack Squire. Such was his modesty about his own achievements, the event took him by surprise. The first speaker was G.K. Chesterton who said of him 'that he would remain for centuries as an example of a man who controlled creative power'. This referred to his influence through the *London Mercury*. But when he was knighted shortly afterwards, it wasn't for his services to literature but for his active part in saving Stonehenge. Patrick Howarth, in his excellent biography *Most Generous of Men* (a tag bestowed on Squire by Siegfried Sassoon), assesses him professionally as 'a good minor poet, a perceptive critic, a brilliant parodist and a great editor.'

Squire married Eileen Wilkinson and they had four children. Someone described him as being 'of medium height, stocky, with no distinction of appearance, but he had a pleasant, friendly face; he was short-sighted and peered at you through heavy lenses. He was untidy and usually looked as though he had shaved with a blunt razor eighteen hours before'. Arnold Bennett described him as 'Jaegerish'. Squire described himself as 'a social centipede with his foot in a hundred worlds.'

But his abiding passion, beyond the odd tot of whisky, was

cricket and his beloved Invalids, which was all the more remarkable since he possessed no real gift for the game. His bowling was better than his batting inasmuch as he bowled longer than he batted. As Captain he was able to do this. He was, of course, Mr Hodge of *England Their England*. To pick up Macdonell's tale:

Having been hit for two sixes, his next ball was not a good one, due mainly to the fact that it slipped out of his hand before he was ready, and it went up and came down in a slow, lazy parabola, about seven feet wide on the leg-side.

It proved too much for the village baker who sprang like a panther, whirled his bat cyclonically, and missed the ball by a foot and a half. The wicket-keeping publisher ... launched a mighty kick at it ... and by an amazing fluke kicked it on to the wicket. Even the ancient umpire had to give the baker out, for the baker was still lying flat on his face outside the crease.

'I was bowling for that,' observed Mr Hodge modestly, strolling up the pitch.

'Too much for the village baker'

1

THE SQUIREARCHY

God heard the embattled nations shout,
Gott straffe England and God save the king,
God this, God that, and God the other thing,
Good God, said God, I've got my work cut out.

This quote from Squire's satirical war verses 'The Survival of
the Fittest' raises the interesting question of how the first
Invalid team came to be picked.

'What are you doing the first Sunday this is all over?'
said a quiet voice to a terrified corporal as all hell was
breaking loose in a dismal, blood-spattered trench somewhere in Flanders. 'I've ... really ... no idea, sir,' replied
the corporal in a soft Scottish brogue.
'You're playing cricket for me.'

And this romantic fable, of Squire's chance meeting with
Archie Macdonell in the heat of battle, was completely blown
apart when Howarth records that Squire took no part in the
fighting, 'being classified as unfit because of poor eyesight,
though he did carry out certain guard duties, in the precincts
of Buckingham Palace.' Added to which, Macdonell went to
Winchester, may not have paraded a Scottish accent and
would, almost certainly, have had a commission.

Richard Butler's research of the first game reveals:

In the Spring of 1920,* a team of authors calling themselves the Old Age Pensioners collected together at West Wycombe (or West Grinstead – some doubt here). The side included the poet Edmund Blunden, later President of the club, who rather surprised his friends by turning up; he had twice been reported killed in action. The scorebook recorded the doleful statistic 'J.C. Squire b Hornung 0.'

But the afternoon must have had its reward because Squire resolved 'his' side would continue. The name was changed to 'The Invalids', team colours to be hospital blue and old gold (the colour of army officers' wartime pyjamas), and the crest a pair of crossed crutches. The war connection, with veterans returning wounded, invalided or otherwise, was thus confirmed.

But the late Mike Seabrook corroborated 1920 and added with firm authority:

The first game arose out of a conversation between Squire and his uncle by marriage, E.W. Hornung, author of *Raffles, the Gentleman Thief*, and brother-in-law of Sir Arthur Conan Doyle, who was himself a fine cricketer. It's on record that Doyle once hit a century for the MCC against Scotland at Lord's, went out to an excellent dinner, and returned home late to polish off a Sherlock Holmes story in time for a sharp deadline for the *Strand Magazine* the next morning. Squire may have rivalled Doyle in regard to the dinner and the deadline, but not on the small matter of the batting.

Hornung played for West Wycombe. A match was arranged.

---

*The first of many confusions this book will throw up. The 50th birthday of the club was celebrated with a dinner at Lord's in 1969; and all subsequent landmarks count back to 1919 as the year of inception.

8

Squire picked his team. 'You can ask,' he wrote, 'the most unlikely, the most aged, decrepit and unpractised of men to play for a scratch team and you will find they are invariably willing ... if a man won't play for any other reason he will play for the sake of a pleasant excursion or because of the exceptional opportunity of raising a thirst.'

Curious adventures inevitably befall a side recruited in this fashion, even and in spite of the efforts of Squire's devoted secretary, Miss Grace Chapman. The first team carried an American called Manning Pike who had never played cricket but knew the rudiments of baseball. Pike was clearly the inspiration for Mr Shakespeare Pollock, the unlikely hero at the climax of Macdonell's tale.

And while on the subject, we can identify some of the real people lurking noticeably behind the fiction of *England Their England*

Alec Waugh, brother of Evelyn, was Bobby Southcott, the 'gentle and almost finicky' novelist who made an eccentric 50. The very stout publisher who crushed Donald Cameron (Macdonell) in the bus and kept wicket with his enormous pads (which did for the baker) was Cecil Palmer.

The fierce Major Hawker who terrified seven batsmen, clean bowled six and broke a stump before retiring to the pub was R.H. Lowe, known as 'the Major' (and for a long time Squire's most reliable opening bowler); and Mr Harcourt, whose bellow of 'no ball' while umpiring unhinged the demon blacksmith, was most probably J.B. Morton (Beachcomber of the *Daily Express*).

Others who played at this time included Clifford Bax, the playwright and brother of Arnold, the composer, A.P. Watt, Squire's literary agent, A.D. Peters, the publisher, W.A. Darlington, theatre critic of the *Daily Telegraph*, A.P. Herbert,

9

Walter Monckton, Hilaire Belloc (some doubt about this), G.K. Chesterton (who once famously sent a telegram to his wife which ran 'Am in Market Harborough, where should I be?' – surely an attempt to locate an Invalid fixture), Hugh Walpole, J.B. Priestley, W.A. Oldfield, the legendary Australian wicket-keeper, P.G.H. Fender (and his daughter)...

...and a youthful Evelyn Waugh who wrote:

My brother (Alec) said to me at breakfast, 'When you last played cricket how many runs did you score?' And I answered him truthfully fifty. I remembered the occasion well for this is what happened.

At school, oh! I had my sixth form privileges taken away for some unpunctuality or other trifling delinquency, and the captain of cricket in my house, a youth with whom I had scarcely ever found myself in sympathy took advantage of my degradation to put me in charge of a game called appropriately a 'remnants game'. I had resented this distinction grimly, but as a matter of fact, the afternoon had been less oppressive than I had expected. Only 21 boys arrived so, there being none to oppose me, I elected to play for both while they were batting. I thus ensured my rest and for an hour or so read contentedly having gone in first and failed to survive the first over. When eventually by various means the whole of one side had been dismissed – the umpire was always the next batsman and, eager for his innings, was usually ready to prove himself sympathetic to the most extravagant appeal – I buckled on the pair of pads a new boy had brought, although they were hotly claimed by the wicket-keeper, and went out to bat. This other side bowled less well and after missing the ball once or twice, I suddenly and to my intense surprise hit it with great force.

10

Delighted by this I did it again and again. The fielding was half-hearted and runs accumulated. I asked the scorer how many I had made and was told '36'. Now and then I changed the bowlers being still captain of the fielding side and denounced those who were ostentatiously slack in the field. Soon I saw a restiveness about both sides and much looking of watches. 'This game shall not end,' I ordained. 'until I have made 50.' Almost immediately the cry came '50' and with much clapping I allowed stumps to be drawn. Such is the history of my only athletic achievement.

On hearing of it my brother said, 'Well you'd better play today, Anderson has just fallen through. We're taking a side down to a village in Hertfordshire – I've forgotten the name.' And I thought of how much I had heard of the glories of village cricket and of that life into which I had never entered and so most adventurously, I accepted.

Be patient, dear reader, for the full account of the ghastly day Evelyn Waugh spends with the Invalids. Some only dreamed of playing.

Neville Cardus wrote that he dreamed he was playing for the Invalids and after half an hour (and he was bowling rather well), it was discovered no-one was keeping the score and so they had to start all over again. The article infuriated Squire, who said (incorrectly) that such a thing could not possibly have happened: Eileen, his wife, always scored; and in any case, Cardus had never played for the Invalids which, in fact, he had not at the time claimed to have done.

It was Cardus who also wrote of the game in which a catch was skied and could have been caught by any one of six Invalid fielders. Squire, captaining from first slip, shouted firmly 'Leave it to Thompson.' But Thompson, alas, wasn't

'Leave it to Thompson'

playing. Squire, again incensed by Cardus, stoutly denied this had ever happened.

Patrick Howarth records that W.T.S. Stallybrass, a cricketer of some ability, was recruited to strengthen the team on a tour of the west country and calculated that he had 39 catches dropped off him in a week, mostly by Squire in the slips, 'where his short-sightedness afforded the maximum handicap.'

To drum the point home, Alec Waugh wrote that Squire was

no cricketer, that he knew he was no cricketer, and that he knew the Invalids knew he was no cricketer, but that everyone was in a conspiracy of silence on the matter. As for his leadership skills, they would surely have interested Mike Brearley, built as they were on steering a match to a point where he could justify giving himself a long bowl. One opposition skipper gave his men firm instructions that nobody was

'He took a four-step trot'

13

to score more than 20 runs in an over off Squire's bowling, for as long as they scored less, he would be under the impression that he was keeping the runs down. Macdonell adds that Mr Hodge (Squire) 'was a poet and therefore a theorist and an idealist. Every ball that he bowled had brain behind it, if not exactness of pitch. He took a four-step trot and tossed high into the air a ball guileless of spin and swerve. It was astonishing how often he broke a partnership.'

Evelyn Waugh continues...

The village we were to play was called Torbridge. At half past twelve we were assembled with many bags on Torbridge platform. Outside two Fords were for hire. We discovered the drivers in the pub, the Horse and Cart. They were very largely sober. My brother said...

   'Drive us to the cricket ground.'
   'There isn't no cricket ground, is there, Billy?'
   'I've heard they do play cricket on Beesley's paddock.'
   'Noa, that's football they plays there.'
   'Ah but that's in winter. Mebbe they plays cricket there in the summer.'
   'I have heard he's got that field for hay this year.'
   'Why, so 'e 'ave.'
   'No, there ain't no cricket ground, mister.'

And then I noticed a signpost. On one limb was written 'Lower Torbridge, Great Torbridge, Torbridge St Swithin' and on the other just 'Torbridge Station' pointing towards me. We tossed up and contrary to the lot, decided to try Torbridge village. We stopped at the only public house there and made enquiries.

   No, they'd not heard of no match here. They did say

there was some sort of festification at Torbridge St Swithin, but maybe that was the flower show.

We continued the pilgimage and at last we found at the Pig and Hammer eleven disconsolate men. They were expecting a team to play them (who hadn't shown up). Would we play them instead? After pints all round the thing was arranged. At a quarter past 4 when we paused for tea, our score was 31 for 7, of these my brother had made 20 in two overs and had then been caught. I had made one and that ingloriously. I hit the ball with great force onto my toe from which it bounced to the middle of the pitch. 'Yes,' said the tall man at the other end; he wanted the bowling; with great difficulty I limped across; I was glad that the next ball bowled him. One man did all the work for the other side – a short man with very brown forearms and a bristling moustache.

At a quarter to 5 we went out to field and at 7, when very wearily we went back to the pavilion, only one wicket had fallen for 120. The brown armed man was still in. And in the field, still with a crushed toe, I had not done myself justice. It became the habit of the bowler whenever a ball was hit near me, immediately to put me somewhere else ; and for this I was grateful.

In the shed at the end of the field there was no way of washing. We had to change in one little room each with his heap of clothes; we all lost socks, studs and even waistcoats. And finally when we were changed and feeling sticky and weary, we learned from the cheery captain with the brown arms that there were no taxis in Torbridge Heath and no telephone to summon one with. It was three miles to the station and the last train left at half past eight...

...As we were coming into King's Cross I found that somewhere in that turmoil of changing I had lost my return ticket. My poor brother had to pay; I having no money. When he had paid he discovered he had no money

15

left for a taxi. To travel by tube at best is an uneasy business, but with a heavy bag of cricket...

When I returned home I reasoned the day thus, that I'd wearied myself utterly; had seen no-one and nothing of any interest; had suffered discomfort in every limb; walked several miles, stood about for several hours, drunken several pints of indifferent beer, and spent nearly two pounds I might have spent in dining well and going to a theatre. But my brother maintained that it had been a great day. 'Village cricket,' he said, 'was always like that.'

There's something mildly suspicious about this story (*Faber Book of Cricket*), credited to Scaramel, pseudonym for the undergraduate Evelyn Waugh, in Cherwell 1923. One isn't questioning Faber, far from it, but the tone suggests a later, more acidic Waugh who, for reasons we shall hit on, detested Squire and all he stood for.

'During the winter (Alec Waugh adds) dinners were held at the Cheshire Cheese. Long clay pipes were smoked, Belloc and Chesterton dropped in and sang like larks,' and Squire finished the evenings with a rousing chorus: 'It'll all be the same, all the same, a hundred years from now.'

Nostradamus couldn't have put it better, if the Invalids carry on as merrily. The only qualification for membership, in those days (as now) was to be a friend of the Captain or a friend of that friend, or if that failed, a local taxi driver.

Early fixtures...

The tradition of getting out of town to play villages was established from the start, the reason being that Squire despised

16

Match played at **Rodmell** on **June 9th** 1923

Innings. **Rodmell**

BATSMEN'S NAMES.	RUNS AS SCORED.	HOW OUT	BOWLER	TOTAL
J. Back		bowled	Waugh	0
R. Parker	1.1.	bowled	Waugh	2
A. Dedman	1.1.1.2.1.1.1.	bowled	Waugh	8
A. Arblaster	1.2.2.	MacDonell	Waugh	5
W. Greenwood	2.1.1.1.	not	out	5
F. Malthouse	2.1.	run	out	3
J. Hubbard	1.2.	bowled	Waugh	3
C. Dean	1.	bowled	Waugh	1
J. Gibbs		bowled	Waugh	0
L. Chantler		bowled	Low	0
A. Thompsett		bowled	Waugh	0
BYES	1.1.1.1.1.			5
LEG BYES				
WIDE BALLS				
NO BALLS				

	1 for	2 for	3 for	4 for	5 for	6 for	7 for	8 for	9 for	10 for	TOTAL	
at the fall of the wicket.	2	3	15	21	22	29	30	30	31			32

RAINEY'S "PROGRESS" SCORE FORM. REGD. No. 78422.

BOWLER.	ANALYSIS OF BOWLING.															No. of Overs.	Maiden Overs.	RUNS.	Wickets	Wide Balls	No Balls	Average per Wicket.
	1	2	3	4	5	6	7	8	9	10	11	12	13	14	15							
Waugh	.:.	W:	M	.:.	M	:.:	W	M	:.:	M	.:.	W	.W			11½	6	7	8			
Peter	:.:	M	:.:	2.:.	.:.	.:.	M	.2.	M	:.:						10	3	19	—			
Low	:.W															1	—	1	1			

The Waugh in question is Alec, not Evelyn!

17

suburban venues (what he called 'trolley-bus' cricket). The journey to and from some of these outposts often provided more drama than the game itself, and it was decided that an Invalid batsman calculated his average, if he shamefully kept such a thing, by dividing the number of runs he scored into the total of miles he travelled; which explains why batsmen of no merit whatever often had averages which soared above even Bradman.

Some of these fixtures are still happily played today, and we shall return to them with relish. But to give a taste, mention can be made of Rodmell near Lewes, which Squire obtained through his friendship with Leonard and Virginia Woolf, who lived there, or else with the landlord of the Abergavenny Arms, a hostelry known to the Invalids to this day. Godfrey Smith of the *Observer* wrote that the square at Rodmell was okay, but the outfield was such a jungle that no score was possible between 1 and 6. A wide swathe was, in earlier days, cut between pavilion and square allegedly so that Sir John could find his way to the wicket.

Some matches had a country house flavour. One was at Tichborne in Hants, presided over by successive Tichborne baronets. Sir Anthony Tichborne's father played to a great age; he was always prepared to bat if required, but he would send his butler out to field for him. If the butler took a catch, it was entered in the scorebook not 'caught sub', but 'caught Tichborne' – in proper feudal style.

Aside from the villages, Squire was not averse to pitting the Invalids' skills against more elevated opposition, sometimes with awkward results. There was a game against the Royal Army Service Corps at Aldershot (writes Patrick Howarth), when Squire sent two of his players as an advance party. One of them, the BBC broadcaster Eric Gillett, had noticed Squire was wearing black patent-leather shoes with his white flannels and regarded this as 'an omen of a bad day ahead.' On arrival they learnt that the RASC included both the Army's opening

18

'Caught Tichborne'

bowlers, and welcomed their visitors with a full military band. The match was supposed to start at 11.30. At 12.30, Squire arrived with four other players, explaining that he had gone to fetch a West Indian who was not to be found. The Invalids batted first, then fielded with four substitutes, Squire spending much of his time despatching telegrams to possible cricketers.

When the match was over and the Invalids had lost by an innings, Squire expressed the opinion that his team had had rather the worse of the luck.

Another occasion against Brasenose College saw an Oxford blue, F.H. Barnard, help himself to 191 off the Invalids' bowling. Before the match, Squire had been indignant to learn the college hadn't found it necessary to field its strongest eleven.

On 29 May 1924, the Invalids played the Lords and Commons at Kennington Oval. The Invalids knocked up 221, with fine efforts from three successful writers (A. Waugh, M.R.K. Burge and C. Bax): and with J.C. Squire, last man, st Hacking b Hogbin 0. The Commons were bundled out for 134 (Lowe 8-58, Peters 3-43) and in their second innings, clearly a knockabout, since Lowe and Peters didn't bowl and the Commons reversed their order, we note that Squire took the wickets of Col. Moore-Brabazon and Sir Rowland Blades for a creditable 60 runs off 11 overs, 0 maidens.

Perhaps the most eccentric of Squire's match fixing, if that is the word these days, was the game played on Broadhalfpenny Down, Hambledon, cradle of cricket, on New Year's Day 1929.

This was against the Hampshire Eskimos, and the motive for it was a resentment that football had invaded the summer months. The spirit in which it was played was described in *The Times* as 'Pickwickian without descending into farce.'

The noted cricket historian, Gerald Howat, writing in *The Times* in 1989, tells the tale...

It was a cold, crisp day with a sky as blue as if on a June morning and a sun casting robust black shadows. A crowd of some 2000 had arrived by car, charabanc, bicycle and shanks's pony, while a lorry had brought a group of Squire's own supporters. All this activity needed a policeman on point duty at Broadhalfpenny Down.

Cinematograph crews and legions of photographers clicked away as Squire tossed up four times with E. Whalley-Tooker, the Eskimos' captain, for their benefit.

Everyone declared that a hundred would be a good score, and Dudley Carew from *The Times* reported, 'a man who made 20 would be a hero'. The Invalids' innings was opened by B. Walton O'Donnell, conductor of the Wireless Military band, who was soon joined by A.D. Peters, the famous literary agent, of whom (Waugh wrote) publishers, editors and authors all stood in awe.

Peters, with 20 runs, qualified for Carew's accolade, and O'Donnell had just failed to when the proceedings were interrupted by the sight of pink huntsmen and the sound of the horn. Major Talbot-Ponsonby, Master of the Hambledon Hunt, had arranged a meet and high up on Hambledon Hill they passed by. It did not take much imagination, Carew thought, to contemplate 'the squat, formidable figure of Squire Osbaldeston among the hunt'; an old print had come to life with square-backed motor cars not far removed from stage-coaches and chauffeurs standing around who might be translated into coachmen.

Soon A.G. Macdonell came to the wicket and, 'although light-heartedly determined on a six', left for a single. R. Strauss had motored down from Scotland across Shap in winter to find himself run out for 1.

Walter Monckton (later Lord Monckton, the barrister and politician who got embroiled in the abdication of a reigning monarch) made 10, and Squire was left 0 not out. Invalids had made 89. Despite the strength of the sun, little remained of the short winter day. The opposition went out immediately to bat. Lowe's bowling suggested 'surreptitious practice' as three Eskimo wickets fell for 9 and they seemed destined to retreat to their igloos in despair. Then one H. Clark became, in Carew's notion of things, a double hero by making 42 and Squire brought

21

on the literary agent and the band conductor, and that ,effectively, was that. Invalids coasted home by 11 runs. Squire's opposite number, Whalley-Tooker, was similarly let not out, a gallant fighter playing in midwinter at the age of 65 and who would turn out against Eton Ramblers later in the year He had had a game for Hampshire in 1882, and perhaps more important, he had revived the old Broadhalfpenny ground where his ancestors had played, and he had had the ploughed-up land returned to a cricket field.

While Howat keeps his eye on the ball, Carew's attention, as might have Henry Blofeld's, lurched back to the hunt.

Across the field they passed, and as they passed and one lost sight of them one knew one had been enriched by an emotional experience which might not betray its full value until the end of many years. After the match had re-started they came once more back clearly to the sight and vigorously to the imagination. Across the fields below the down they went streaming after a fox found as conveniently as though it had been carried in the pocket of the whip.

After the match, when the Bat and Ball proved a sad deceiver, everyone repaired to the George for supper. And the last word must go to Sir John himself, who wrote:

It was over before tea-time. The wind grew increasingly bitter and nobody had the temerity to suggest a second innings. Gradually the cars and the charabancs melted away and the down relapsed into solitude. But the proceedings were not over. Anybody who has read Mr E.V. Lucas's delightful book, *The Hambledon Men*, knows that they, who could cope with All England on the cricket

22

field, were equally capable of coping with All England when it came to eating and drinking. It is to be feared that the 18th century dinners ended rather more bibulously than is the modern habit.

But at that famous old hostelry, the George at Hambledon, the two teams, the umpires and certain supporters did their poor 20th century best. Every sort of suitable health was drunk. A song, composed by Mr Peter Warlock, to rollicking words by Mr G.H.B. Blunt, was rendered at frequent intervals. The company then removed themselves to a delightful upper chamber, with roaring open fires. Here the Hambledon Brass band, which had been playing 'John Peel' and such tunes with unabated vigour all day on the blasted heath, were sitting in their peaked caps, with their immense trombones and bombardons, ready to renew the fray. In the presence of Mr B. Walton O'Donnell, probably the best military band conductor in the world, they rose to the occasion, assisted by an occasional moistening draught, playing every tune they were asked for. Finally, the cornet soloist gave a magnificent rendering of 'The Lost Chord'.

Would the fixture become an annual event? No.

'It is always a mistake to endeavour to repeat perfection,' Squire said firmly.

The early thirties...

David Money, a fine wicket-keeper batsman, who has just given up playing in his eighties, has a collection of letters which typifies the way the Invalids set about arranging their fixtures. To avoid total confusion, they are listed in chronological order.

27 October 1932

On a card headed *The London Mercury, A Monthly Review of Literature & the Arts, Edited by J.C. Squire*, this note was written to Malcolm Elwin, the writer who contributed to the magazine and was captain of North Stoke in Oxfordshire.

Awfully sorry to have to cancel our match, but we have decided in view of various difficulties to abandon cricket and confine ourselves to dining in the winter.' (Signed by Grace Chapman in her handwriting for Invalids C.C.)

P.S. No money yet, but you are high on the accountants list.

5 November 1932

A letter written to Malcolm Elwin at North Stoke, signed Major (assumed to be R.H. Lowe).

My dear Elwin

Many thanks for your letter. I quite agree with you that the Invalids must not be allowed to fall into the jaws of extinction. I will see to it that a strong purge is administered! Quite a simple but generally effective remedy for those suffering from debility, prostration, and other nervous disorders!! I think Jack's exploits – 4.30 arrival etc., at your home match – rather put the tin hat on things! However I have made enquiries and think that Powell-Jones will take over the responsibility of raising and running the side. So keep our fixture with you; for if anyone else failed I would very gladly raise a side – at least for you and the Douai people. It would be dreadful to think of dropping these very welcome and jolly games. I suppose you won't be in town on Tuesday – Nov 15th – the Invalids supper at the Cheshire Cheese? I found – much to my surprise – that Miss Chapman has left Jack and retired to the country. Perhaps this event finally convinced Jack of his helplessness!!

16 December 1932

Letter to Elwin on *London Mercury* notepaper.

Dear Sir,
    Will you be good enough to arrange for North Stoke to play the Invalids on July 1st, 1933, as I find this is one of our vacant dates ... please confirm this at your convenience. Yours faithfully p.p. THE INVALIDS C.C.

9 January 1933

From the *London Mercury* to Elwin.

Dear Sir,
    Thank you for your letter of the 7th instant. Yes, the Invalids can come to North Stoke on either of the first two Saturdays in July, so I have altered the fixture to July 8th, start at noon. Yours truly, p.p THE INVALIDS C.C.

3 June 1933 (sic. But posted exactly a month later)

Mercury to Elwin.

Dear Sir,
    Since writing you this morning, I have found great difficulty in raising an eleven for Saturday's match. This is mainly due to Clifford Bax's annual match at Seaford. I will wait until Tuesday mid-day to see if things improve; if they do not I will send you a telegram, reluctantly having to scratch.
                    Yours faithfully, THE INVALIDS C.C.

No wonder Miss Chapman fled to the country; and whether this game actually took place is in doubt. But Elwin received the following note four months later:

7 November 1933

Dear Sir,
   Many thanks for your letter of Oct 31. I have booked July 7th for the Invalids visit to North Stoke next year, starting at 2 o'clock. Yours very truly p.p. THE INVALIDS C.C.

However, a report in the *Oxford Times* describes the match the previous summer, 1932, which had clearly prompted the Major's letter to Elwin (see above):

North Stoke v Invalids (Mr J.C. Squire's XI)

North Stoke ... batting first, ran up their best score of the season − 277-5. Although the bowling was good, runs came steadily, 25 being on the board when H.J. Madgwick was bowled and 55 when Harold Madgwick left (unfortunately run out). On R. Birch being joined by his captain (M. Elwin) a prolonged stand was made, and when at last a separation was effected, the outgoing batsman (Birch) had scored 75 (total 147). A. Stevenson was next to leave after collecting 57 which included five 6's. M. Elwin was not got rid of until he had scored 76. When the visitors went in they fared badly against the bowling of G. Madgwick and T. Allaway, the former capturing 5 wickets for 15 runs. Mr Squire's XI, who come every year from London for the fixture, were entertained to lunch by Mr H. Hartley, and to tea by Mrs Malcolm Elwin.

26

One or two points of interest emerged from the scorecard. Elwin was a superbly accurate late inswing bowler (he opened the bowling for Oxfordshire and for Devon in his prime) who seldom batted higher than 10 or 11. Here he batted 4 and was bowled Lowe 76: Birch was st Ryan b Squire 75 (the rare sighting in print of a Squire wicket); and in the Invalids total of 59 all out, Elwin didn't bowl and Squire didn't bother to bat.

Malcolm Elwin, through his connection with Squire, turned out occasionally for the Invalids. Indeed they inspired him to form his own team with Stephen Fry (C.B.'s son) called the South Oxfordshire Amateurs, which has built a fine reputation for itself over the years. But the harsh truth is that Elwin avoided like the plague anything which might be termed a 'literary establishment'. In David Money's witty history *Fifty Years Of The SOA* we find this quote from Elwin in the *Nottingham Journal*, 'I've always preferred cricketers to writers for company – with a few exceptions.'

Letter to Elwin, dated 22 May 1934, Stephen Fry writes, 'I was playing yesterday with Caulfield for the Invalids, near Godalming ... disastrous match for the Invalids!'

Postscript. In the Festival for Wandering Clubs worldwide in Oxford in August 2000, conceived by Geoffrey Hartley and *The Cricketer International*, the SOA were drawn to play, for the first time ever, the Invalids on the St Edwards School ground. The result? A fairly presentable Invalids side (without a writer in sight) was effortlessly despatched by 80-odd runs.

'Good God, said God ...' Squire on the subject of Women in Cricket in a letter to *The Times*, 16 April 1938.

Sir, it is pleasant to see your Cricket Correspondent sticking to his guns about women's Test cricket. He has put

27

'Disastrous match for the Invalids'

his thumb on the right spot. I, too, saw the Oval Test match. I was as surprised as he, but I admitted these facts; namely, that the two teams fielded better than some first class county sides and produced a lovely variety of strokes from straighter bats than are now common, and had bowlers who kept a length, both slow and (by any standard) very nearly fast. I have since been informed by diehards who 'weren't there' (a) politely, 'You are exaggerating' or 'You must be romantic about women' or (b) impolitely, 'They are only fit to play with men playing left-handed with broomsticks' or 'You are talking through your hat'. In answer, I say women can not only bat but they can <u>throw</u>. These 'girls' picked up and threw in from the boundary with an accuracy which would have done credit to a University side, and the knowledgeable Oval crowd duly recognized it. They were on their toes all the time and some of the catches were miraculous: there was one Australian 'girl' who took a somersalt catch which I have never seen bettered at Lord's. There were shots through the covers and fizzing square cuts for 4 which reminded one of former days.

They play with a ball slightly smaller than men's size. That is reasonable; on the average their hands are smaller, though there was at least one pair of hands on the field which looked like hip-baths compared with my own. They hit no 6; they had obviously been trained to keep the ball on the ground, they had not the size or 'beef' of Mr Percy Fender; there were one or two hits that might have got a 6 by the tavern at Lord's; but the Oval is a very big ground, as anybody (like myself) who has had to walk from the wicket to the pavilion after making a duck in a humble holiday match well knows.

I stick with my view that either team might have beaten some of our county sides. Not our best; brawn counts.

29

But cricket is coming into line with the other games. Mlle Suzanne Lenglen was no better than some men, but she was better than most men. Miss Joyce Wethered might not have been able to beat some of the male golfers of her time, but she could have taken on most of them, as I am sure that your Golf Correspondent will bear me out.

Yours faithfully,

J.C. Squire.

So far as is known, only five 'girls' have turned out for the Invalids: (1) Mr P.G.H. Fender's daughter, an enchanting young actress (whom the playwright, Ben Travers* cast in one of his famous Aldwych farces starring Robertson Hare and Ralph Lynn); (2) The daughter of your guide, the enchanting Sophie, who won an Oxford half Blue in 1991 and once outscored her father in a partnership of 3 against the Pink Elephants in Vincent Square; (3) A Polish Countess (of whom more later); (4) A girl with the enchanting name of Pandora (more later); and (5) a mysterious girl called simply 'Anne' found in a scorebook batting 10 on 23 June 1963 at Cowden. (She scored 4 not out.)

---

*There's no record of Travers having ever played for the Invalids, but he should have. His love of cricket was legendary; he would follow England on every overseas tour, regardless of work commitments. He wrote a highly successful play *The Bed Before Yesterday* after his ninetieth year. His agent eagerly awaited his next one, but had to concede that the old boy had finally flipped his lid when the first stage direction read: 'Enter a thousand elephants'.

Another who imbibed the Invalid spirit was the stage and screen actor, Trevor Howard, who had it written into all his film contracts that he was unavailable for work when England were playing a Test Match anywhere in the world. This led to the occasion when he flew in from a film location in Northern Australia in time for the first ball at Lord's, only to be barred entry into the pavilion because he wasn't wearing any socks.

2

THE SURVIVAL OF THE FITTEST

If Trevor Howard helped win the war with his appearances on the silver screen, Squire also played his part, but with more of a walk-on role. He was 55 when war broke out, and his fortunes were at a low ebb. His original work was drying up, his marriage was over, and he was drifting around London. But he rallied, volunteering for service in the Home Guard, where he was reputed to be enthusiastic and diligent and determined not to drink while on duty. The image of Captain Mainwaring in *Dad's Army* springs to mind. Arthur Lowe, Captain of the Invalids? Not too fanciful, but there was no time for cricket. The carefree days of bucolic bliss and bibulous levity, which Sir John had done so much to inspire, seemed gone for good, lost in a haze; and since everything rested with its founder, the future of the Invalids hung by a thread.

The Markham Arms: Summer 1945...

Young Patrick Howarth, still in uniform, is sitting with a group of friends in a well-known Chelsea pub. The conversation is cricket and how they might start up a team. The door opens and a figure enters. 'There's your captain,' someone says.

Squire's hair is white, his hands shake badly, but his eyes are 'puckish' and his face is radiant as plans are hatched to revive the Invalids. Howarth recalls the first match as a

31

'The survival of the fittest'

virtual re-run of Macdonell's fictional account all those years before. By coincidence, the village is Fordcombe in Kent, which cannot be too far from the legendary Fordenden.

I'd taken the precaution of enlisting Ian Akers-Douglas, who had played cricket for Cambridge and Kent. The

Fordcombe score was something like 220 for 3 dec. This was understandable, as Squire had done a good deal of the bowling. Our score was 67 all out. Of these Akers-Douglas made 42, I made 19, with several extras. Not the least competent of our performers were a Polish squadron-leader and a Russian portrait painter.

Of the pre-war team it seems only Howarth, Edmund Blunden, Ian Leslie and Sir John himself swapped their uniforms for flannels. There must have been others, but they have vanished into the mists. Alec Waugh had lost touch and assumed the Invalids were done for. He was delighted to be corrected, and was an honoured guest at the 60th anniversary dinner at the Turf Club in 1979.

The Invalids, by their very name, had sprung into life as the result of war. It is fine to suppose that they were formed as an aid to recovery from broken limbs and broken spirits, though the truth may be less exalting. We find no testimonies from anyone from either war who played with a physical handicap, who had suffered gas or carried shrapnel or whose life had been mentally scarred. It seems that a day in the country with Squire and his men blanked out such matters.

But the new recruits in the late 40s and early 50s were in fact carrying war experience of varying intensity. Among these were Bill Foss, Edward Bishop and Tom Tatham, who recall their introductions and raise a glass to some old colleagues.

Bill Foss...

I'd served in SOE's Force 136 in the Far East. I came home and met up with Tim Jenkins (a friend from Oxford) and Patrick Dalmahoy. One spent quite a bit of one's time in the Antelope in those days. I got involved

33

with the team because I had a motor car. That was the key. I was asked one day if I was doing anything, I said no and they said, would I care to come, not to play cricket but to drive them to cricket? Then they said would I score for them? I said yes, I enjoyed the company. Was I a cricketer myself? Yes, but that had nothing to do with it, until they found they were short and said would I care to play? I went in 11. That's how things were in those days.

Foss on Tim Jenkins...

He was a left-handed bat, a bit stodgy but determined: a Yorkshire Grammar School boy who got to Keble College, Oxford. He joined the Army, got a commission, didn't like it, so he joined the Air Force, got a commission, didn't like that; so he joined the Navy. He was probably the only sailor who before his commission wore RAF wings. He ended up on D-Day as he told me, 'driving one of those things with chaps across the channel and landing them in France. I got 'em there and turned the bloody thing back and got out as fast as I could!' After the war, he joined Unilever, prospered, but thought he was wasting his talents so went to Hong Kong. He came back and bought a bar in Ibiza, spending most of his time on the customer side. Finally he took a pub at Thame, where he finished his days rather sadly.

Foss's first memory of Squire?

Jenkins introduced me and, being a newcomer keen to make an impression, I said, 'Would you like a drink, Sir John?' 'Yes, thank you, double brandy.' So I got him a double brandy and Jenkins told me what a fool I'd been, but I could have been let off lightly. Bishop said that the first words Sir John spoke to him on introduction were...

'Quadruple whisky,' pushing an empty tumbler towards me. (*Bishop recalls*) 'Of course I felt obliged to comply, and for the first and last time bought him a quadruple whisky and one for myself. I soon learned doubles were just as acceptable.'

The writer Edward Bishop reflects on his journey from battle to cricket field...

In the winter of 1946–47 I returned from Singapore where I'd been a war reporter on *SEAC*, the daily inter-service newspaper started in Calcutta by Mountbatten. I'd been recruited for this by Frank Owen, former editor of the *Evening Standard*, who was masquerading as a Lt-Col. The fact that I was serving on HMS *Stevenstone* fighting E-boats in the Channel and bombarding Normandy beaches on and after D-Day didn't bother him. As a former Liberal MP he knew A.V. Alexander, First Lord of the Admiralty, who removed me from *Stevenstone* and had me posted to Calcutta. Getting there in the autumn of 1944 wasn't easy, but I hitched a lift on a troopship, the *Sanfoin*, arrived in Bombay and caught a train to Calcutta.

Not perhaps relevant to the Invalids, excepting that the spirit of the early post-war matches was very much influenced by the freebooting war some of us had had. We tended to play as we'd fought, though nobody spoke about it much at the time; perhaps because we were trying to build civilian careers. But apart from the team's drinking ethos set by our founder, which some of us felt we had to live up to and enjoyed in the process (to our various forms of distress in later life), the Invalids

35

provided an opportunity to carry on drinking, so often the relief from war-imposed stress.

In September, 1945 Bishop had helped to get cricket going again on the Padang, the Singapore Cricket Club's splendid ground between the municipal and court buildings and the sea.

We harnessed a team of Jap POWs to an enormous heavy roller and drove them into repairing the ravages of occupation. The SCC's pavilion, I discovered, had been occupied by the Kempetei (the Jap version of the Gestapo) who, finding cricket bats discarded by murdered or imprisoned members, had used them to bash people up. I liberated a new Don Bradman bat in perfect condition apart from bloodstains and indentations which had been covered with binding. Soon I was opening the bowling for Singapore – which enabled me to boast international status when I joined the Invalids.

Just after the war, the writer Ian Fleming, then foreign manager of Kemsley Newspapers (*Sunday Times* and other titles) got Bishop to join his staff, after his reporting of the trials and first hangings of Japanese war criminals at Changi Jail for the *Singapore Free Press*. On his return home in 1947, Bishop was having a beer in a Knightsbridge pub when he was accosted by...

... a boozy, gentlemanly fellow who asked if I played cricket. Yes, for Singapore. ***Richard Longman***, younger brother of Mark, head of the publishing firm, introduced me to the Invalids the next day. Richard was a stylish batsman of languid Etonian stance who seldom turned

36

out, being usually too much the worse for wear to reach the match. He faded from the scene, dying quite young.

My first match was probably at West Wycombe on Dashwood land and scene of the Hellfire Club. Most of us travelled to matches by train. Few had cars. Even **Brian Kemp**, the future multi-millionaire, and his wife **Joy** were train people. Brian, a former Warrant Officer pilot, became almost certainly the wealthiest Invalid through his partnership with **Walter Flack**, a Jewish ex-Army sergeant. Starting as Flack, Furness and Kemp, estate agents, they prospected prime high street sites for such as Sainsbury and Marks and Spencer. This blossomed into Murrayfield Estates and then City Centre Properties with developments in New York. Flack died fairly young. I seem to remember he was found dead in a bath of champagne aboard his yacht at Cadogan Pier ... surrounded by naked girls.

Brian and Joy Kemp...

They were the life and soul of the train journeys where time was passed with hilarious spelling bees, singsongs and childish games with intermittent peeing out of the window as we returned to London full of beer. As the Kemps prospered they bought The Park at Wisborough Green in Sussex. Brian prepared a cricket ground in his parkland, with deer taking a haughty interest on the boundaries. Beer barrels were rolled out and there was a lot of fun. Everything came in barrels at The Park, even whisky, gin and rum were on tap. Later the Kemps bought a house in Eaton Terrace, Belgravia. They were particular friends of Sir John's eldest son, **Raglan Squire**, who had a hand in re-developing Eaton Square and environs in the postwar property revival.

Dougie Ashpool...

Our favourite fixture was Outwood in Surrey where Dougie, a hopeless cricketer and wonderful host, welcomed us generously. His team were a mixture of toffs and village. After he once bought a round for £6, one of his yokels marvelled 'that's more than my week's wage.' Dougie was the owner of Ashpool and Twiddy, Leicestershire knitwear manufacturers, and he put our somewhat ragged outfit to shame with his immaculate whites and blancoed boots. He feigned the Percy Fender amateur country cricketer style and affected a Douglas Jardine neckerchief and stance as he directed his field. But it was all performance. He was no good! An ardent Surrey supporter, he employed Jim Laker as a knitwear salesman at his showroom near the BBC.

Over the years Dougie and Gladys (nee Twiddy) became great friends of ours, and Tim Jenkins and I often stayed at the Manor House. One night Squire was there too. We were awakened at six one morning by a noise in the garden. Opening the bedroom window, we saw Sir John prowling the borders. Ashpool asked him if he needed anything and had he any preference for breakfast? 'Oh, don't go to any trouble. Just a light one.'

'Lightly boiled egg?' Dougie enquired. 'No, you fool. A light ale of course.'

The Antelope pub and George Canham...

...the rosy and rotund landlord was a father to his 'boys', who presented him with a clock recording our names. It hung over the door leading to the stairs down to the lavatory for many years. The subscribers included little *George Cruickshank* and big *Bill Law*. Some nights as pints multiplied George would get characteristically stroppy. This was a signal for Bill, a vast former marine and fine rugby player for London Scottish, to pick George up and hang him, stranded and legs kicking, from a coat hook. George, whatever his private thoughts about this, took it all in good part. At work he was an industrious and successful director of the advertising agency Foot, Cone and Belding.

Tom Tatham takes up the baton, but first a word of introduction.

Tom joined the Invalids in 1950 at the tail-end of the Squire-archy. Until his recent death, he was their most venerated supporter. This accolade was bestowed on him in 1998, when after an arduous drive made by his dear wife Nancy from their Lewes home to Underriver in Kent, it was found on arrival that Tom's wheelchair had no chance of mounting the stile which led to any decent view of the game. The Tathams had the single option of returning directly to Lewes; a round trip of five hours on a hellish road on a blazing hot summer day.

Tatham first draws attention to Squire's batting (*cf Conan Doyle's*)...

The opposition, when bowling to him, moderated the force of their deliveries. But he was once struck painfully amidships. 'Don't you wear a box, Sir John?' someone inquired solicitously. 'No, it interferes with my sprinting between the wickets.'

39

And, on the subject of Squire's captaincy, Tatham recalls...

Once, at Brook, we had playing for us (I can't imagine why), a West Indian Test Match bowler, *C.R. Browne*. It was naturally assumed he would open the bowling, but Sir John had the poetic idea to hold Browne in reserve, to go through the tail. With the score at 165 for 2 an hour before tea, it was quietly acknowledged the ploy had been unsuccesful. Another time, at Rodmell, I felt myself victimised. Sir John had gone off at tea to visit his old friend Leonard Woolf, and I was enjoying the unusual luxury of a fairly long bowl. At six o'clock, Squire marched on to the field and instantly took me off, to show who was in charge.

On women's cricket, Tatham carries a personal grievance:

I was once given out LBW at Balcombe by a lady umpire when I was some way down the wicket.

This raises the point that a man stomping back to the pavilion furious at an LBW decision (whether given by a lady or an ignorant team mate or a passing giraffe), having so misjudged the ball as to miss it, how can he possibly know that it wouldn't have hit his wicket?

Tatham now pays gracious homage to the Invalids' first 'professional' umpire.

He was only known as *Mr Mackley* and was recruited by Squire in a London pub. His main advantage was that he was a railway pensioner so, in the days of petrol rationing, he could travel free on the trains. That he was a good umpire was confirmed by a remark he made to an opposing captain when asked if he was the Invalids' umpire.

40

'No, sir, I am umpiring a match in which the Invalids are playing.'

He had his own dislikes about various grounds. Someone upset him at Brook ... but he favoured Outwood and made them a set of ashtrays constructed of bottle tops which remained long in use. He had an unusual vocabulary. Roger Gray QC once met him in the street in March and Mr Mackley said, 'Oh, I am looking forward to the summer when we all go down into the country and Sir John corroborates the cuckoo.' At one time he'd worked on the French Railways and was proud of his command of that language. 'Howzat?' 'Pas sortie,' he was equipped to say, though it might have been met with a baffled stare depending on the bowler's parley-vous. He took a poor view of the state of English Test Cricket (circa 1950), muttering it was the fault of the MCC and 'that Lord Hawke', being unaware his lordship had died some years earlier.

Mr Mackley died one winter with a rumour persisting that Squire owed him a fair amount of 'expenses'. When challenged by this, Squire cracked open a bottle of champagne to express his gratitude to a fine and loyal friend to the club, and the question of money went begging.

More Tatham recollections...

At Outwood, Squire joined some friends in a car who had a supply of brandy, and his concentration on the game slackened slightly. As wickets began to fall an Invalid hurried over to tell Sir John he was in next. Though surprised, he was equal to the occasion. Putting his head out of the car window, he announced, 'I declare.'

Coming home late from a match, Sir John was in need of relief, and grumbling furiously because the public

41

conveniences were all closed at 11 pm. 'It's a perfect scandal,' he said, 'but not the sort of thing you can write to *The Times* about.'

'The good old habit of tying them up with a tie had failed him'

About the celebrated occasion when Squire's trousers fell down there are conflicting accounts. Eric Warburg, an eyewitness, reports:

I have a vivid memory of a game against Brook on their delightful ground in Surrey. They had put in two young opening batsmen who were soon well over 100 for 0 and going strong; we later found out they were minor county players. Sir John had been put out of harm's way at long leg, but he was still having a testing time from the onslaught. We were never sure whether he saw the ball coming towards him, so had to shout to warn him. On one occasion we all shouted 'Yours, Sir John,' and when he had focused on the ball he started to waddle towards it, but on the way over, his trousers fell down. The good old habit of tying them up with a tie had failed him.

Tatham begs to differ on a point of detail. Responding to a letter in the *Daily Telegraph* on the subject, he claims it contained an inaccuracy:

It was suggested at the time of the mishap, Sir John was hurrying keenly after the ball. At this point of his career, Sir John *never* hurried after the ball. He was in fact in his customary static pose which made the descent of his trousers all the more remarkable.

Tatham continues:

Once, in a match somewhere in North London (trolleybus cricket) Squire spotted a signpost to Potter's Bar and Ponders End, and with a flash of the old poetic spirit he reeled off the refrain 'Where Potter kept his bar and

43

Ponder met his end'. It might have been the match he fixed in a pub encounter, against Telfer's Meat Pies. The hosts spared no pains, and on arrival at the ground, the Invalids were greeted by a banner 'Welcome to Sir John Squire and the Invalids'. An all-day match ensued with a good lunch provided, but, curiously, no meat pies on the menu.

Tatham's early team mates included...

Ian Leslie, the architectural journalist and wicket-keeper who stood up to fast bowlers until a late age. He had been a notable amateur boxer with the Belsize Club and served on MCC sub-committees. He later became President of the Invalids. *Myles Eadon* played for Oxford without quite getting a blue, and *Martin Meeson* appeared for Cambridge under Ted Dexter, an experience he hadn't enjoyed. *Adrian Ames* kept wicket and was noted for the fierce vigour with which he returned the ball to the bowlers. He always travelled his darts with him for after-match competition in the pub.

Norman Neale, another keeper who 'continued to climb in the Himalayas when most people would have been satisfied with Primrose Hill', recalls a Squire incident...

It was at Tichborne, and a convivial day had ended with Sir John being put to bed in the manor. He woke in the middle of the night remembering he had an article to write. He came downstairs still in his cricket sweater, but no trousers. A maid saw him and shrieked, at the moment Lady Tichborne arrived home from an evening engagement. Sir John was despatched on the first available train back to London and never invited again.

Edward Bishop remembers his friend, Roger Gray, QC...

He was an exceedingly stylish batsman who, but for the war, would have played for Oxford, possibly a county, but Invalids cricket and drinking suited his freewheeling style. Although he became a Silk, the Lord Chancellor (Hailsham) stopped short of offering him the High Court place he merited. Knowing too much of his Bohemian ways and extramarital relationships, he allowed him to sit only as a Deputy Judge. What finally ditched his elevation (to his wife Ann's fury) was his discovery by the Lord Chief Justice at an inappropriate moment standing on his head and drinking a pint of beer. Another party trick was song and dance with boater and cane *à la* Maurice Chevalier.

Gray died in 1992, aged 71. *The Times* **obituarist describes his war and after:**

He was commissioned into the Royal Artillery and served with the Ayrshire Yeomanry, 151st Field Regiment in Normandy. Ten days after D-Day he landed with 25-pounder guns of the 11th Armoured Division, and took part in the fierce 'Operation Goodwood' fighting for Hill 112 as Montgomery's forces sought a break-through East of Caen. Later he was involved in the taking of Antwerp. He was promoted Captain and embarked for India after VE Day, serving as GSO 3 (military operations) at GHQ where he was recognised as an outstanding staff officer. Before repatriation his adventurous spirit led him into a hazardous expedition in Ladakh along the Kashmir-Tibet borders.

He returned to Oxford in 1947 and was President of the Union, before being called to the Bar. In court he was by turns stubborn and flamboyant, with something of Rumpole about him. His most sensational engagement was in 1974, when he acted as counsel for the 'Spanking Colonel', a former Mayor of Kensington and Chelsea, suing the *Sunday People* over allegations that he was a menace to young women. The main witness for the defence was a young lady said to have been trapped aboard the Colonel's cabin cruiser on the Thames where she was forced to undress and be spanked and then suffer the further indignity of being doused in whisky to prevent bruising. The Colonel never denied his predilection, 'I am and always have been perfectly normal,' he thundered, after admitting that he had spanked several girls 'in friendly horseplay'. He maintained that he never touched anyone's bottom against their will and always made a point of paying for his pleasure. Gray robustly argued the Colonel's case, observing that 'every full-blooded, healthy, normal, vigorous male is a bottom-slapper in mind if not in the deed. The crime, if any, was pouring whisky over the girl, which will horrify Scotsmen'. The colonel won his case and was awarded a halfpenny in damages.

The Times obituarist concludes…

…his elegant batting might have earned him an honoured place in *Wisden* … but he was most at home with the Invalids, the wandering club founded by the peripatetic (if not paralytic) poet and essayist Sir John Squire and immortalised in A.G. Macdonell's classic book *England Their England*.

46

Another irrepressible character was Oliver Moxon, whose traditional cricketing attire was always accentuated by a pair of scarlet-red socks. Bishop recounts...

Ollie had been a pilot in Burma and written a novel trilogy starting with *The First Monsoon*, the books based on wartime jungle flying. At about this time he started Book Express, a warehouse and distribution business which flourished so much that a little-known entrepreneur named Captain Robert Maxwell MC (trading on his heroics) bought Ollie out for £20,000. The Maxwell empire was thus built on 'Invalid' foundations.

Tatham picks up on Moxon...

After Maxwell, he abandoned train travel and used to arrive at matches in a second-hand Rolls-Royce.
At Abinger, Squire was leading his team forcefully out to field and he said to Moxon, 'Oliver, you take the covers.' 'Yes, Sir John, where shall I put them?' It was Moxon who produced the Polish Countess. They were 'fielding' together in the long grass at deep square leg when the Countess was surprised by the ball hitting her. Moxon grabbed it, hurled it in, ran the batsman out and returned to his fielding position.

Moxon also owned a restaurant, for a while, in Farnham; and invented for fun the story of a puma running wild in the neighbourhood, which was kept up for weeks by a gullible Press. Like Squire before him, Moxon had a nibble at politics. He failed to get the Tory nomination at Goole, admitting that, at the time of presenting himself, he hadn't been entirely sober. He switched to the Liberals but lost his deposit in Hove. Later he became a JP, which bemused his friends who couldn't

'Oliver, you take the covers'

see him dispensing Justice from the Bench. He finally gave up the Invalids when he thought they were taking things too seriously.

Simon Collins, a current Invalid of style and panache, speaks of his late father, Michael, who joined the war survivors who were setting the character of the team at this time.

He fought the Japanese as a Major in the Indian Army and stayed on for partition in 1947. From there he worked in Singapore for the shipping company, Bousteads. He met my mother, Marcia, in Bangalore. They were married in 1949 but, like many returning to England and civilian life, my father's life wasn't easy. He was pleased to meet up with some old friends at the Antelope (Foss, Dalmahoy and Jenkins) who introduced him to Squire's happy band of revellers, which did much to smooth his path.

In 1960, my father, working now in the paper industry, asked Alec and Eric Bedser to play for the Invalids. All was set for the two cricketing giants to join the panoply of stars, war heroes, theatricals and good-egg no-hopers that make the Invalids what they are ... and the fixture was rained off!

My father died in 1985 and many stories have gone with him to the grave, but my mother remembers after a happy game at Underriver (in 1957) being led to the bedside of a frail Sir John Squire, with a bottle of whisky in hand, to aid conversation.

Tatham recalls some actors...

The only ex-county cricketer who played regularly was an amiable elderly actor called Humphrey Kent who had turned out for Middlesex in the early 20s. Though past his best, he would produce strokes which gave evidence of his early prowess. He was sometimes known as the pantomime horse, because it was understood that he annually enacted that part, or at least part of it, at Windsor rep.

Other actors at this time included Godfrey Kenton and Bill Shine, neither of them cricketers but both 'good companions and raconteurs'. Tatham says of Shine:

He'd arrive rather tardily at matches, driven by his wife in an aged three-wheeler. He seldom played large parts but was always in work because he turned up on time, managements liked him and found him no trouble.

Tatham's opinion of actors could also be rather brusque.

There was one who supplemented his earnings by appearing in adverts. One showed a photograph of him executing a perfect forward stroke of a type unfamiliar to all who had ever played with him. He went to Alf Gover's school in the winter and considered the ad made him a fine batsman. He said he would only play for the Invalids if he was put in first. This led me to declare that I would only play for the Invalids if I was put in last.

And Tony Hancock...

...he had obviously been a good cricketer, but he wasn't popular because people queued up in pubs to get his autograph. His departure from the Invalids was unfortunate. We were playing against the Ancient Mariners and a high catch went up. No-one called out a name and Hancock and Struan Robertson, an excellent man from what was then Rhodesia, both went for it and collided. Hancock was a heavy man and Struan's jaw was broken, while Hancock suffered a minor injury to his knee. While Struan was taken off to hospital in the back of a little white van, the door of which wouldn't shut, the spotlight stayed firmly on Hancock. The great comedian was in a fret because he had an appointment the next day with his scriptwriters which he thought he'd be unable to keep. He never played for the Invalids again.

Tatham has happier memories of the actor Bill Franklyn.

Bill was a quick bowler who had trials for Essex. He'd been recruited from the Stage CC. Once, he was resting peacefully at first slip, and Robin Mudie, skippering and usually the most easy-going of men, felt obliged to tell him to wake up! The very next ball the batsman edged to second slip, who promptly grassed it. 'There, you see,' said Bill to the world at large, 'I get the bollocking, he drops the catches'.

Bishop adds this about Franklyn...

With a bounding, leaping and altogether theatrical run-up of a kangaroo, he was regarded as a latter-day Spofforth. The fact that I had recently returned from Australia and I had practised in the Sydney nets with Test players of the day (to get stories as a correspondent) supported my claim to open the bowling – until Bill, watched by his fan Anthony Newley, superseded me!

Franklyn is still playing with all his old zest, having cannily converted to leg-spin and late order swiping. He runs a team called The Sargent's Men, named after Sir Malcolm Sargent. They play at the Bank of England ground at Roehampton, and they've raised thousands of pounds over the years in charity games for children's cancer.

51

Invalids Beat Wisden's
Memorial Match at Lewes

(Extract from the *Sussex Daily News* 1950)

The mayor of Lewes (Ald. H.E. Parrish) was yesterday presented with three Wisden cricket bats, each auto-graphed by Denis Compton 'to use at his discretion.'

The presentation was made by Mr P.J. Chaplin, chair-man of John Wisden & Co. at a luncheon which preceded a cricket match between the firm's team and Sir John Squire's well-known team 'The Invalids'. The match was arranged to celebrate the centenary of the firm which was founded by John Wisden, son of a Brighton builder who became known as the 'little wonder' of cricket. In reply to a toast to the Borough of Lewes, Ald. Parrish said that it was hoped that in a few years Lewes would have a county cricket ground, one of the finest in Sussex...

The Mayor of Brighton (Ald. S. Davey) proposed a toast to all Invalids ... Mr Edmund Blunden responding recalled that John Wisden in 1850 clean bowled all 10 Northern batsmen in an innings at Lord's...

Sir John Squire, giving a toast to 'cricket and the little wonder', pointed out that Edmund Blunden, playing today, had been a member of the first ever Invalid team...

A message of good wishes to Wisden's was received from Denis Compton...

And the match itself?

Invalids batted first and lost five wickets for only 34 runs. Then Eadon and Harris carried the score to 116. The innings was declared at 136-9...

The Wisden batsmen fared badly against the bowling of

R. Gray (3-12), A. Boyd (2-8) and M. Eadon (5-57), and the side were all out for 89.

Some individual batting performances catch the eye: Ian Leslie 0, Roger Gray 9, Miles Eadon 46, Humphrey Kent 9, Alastair Boyd 0, Brian Kemp 7, Oliver Moxon 1, Edmund Blunden not out 2 ... Sir John Squire did not bat.

Sir John – the Closing Overs...

The pleasure Squire took from the revival of his team was enormous. The regular sessions in the Antelope pub, in the company of people who were hard-drinking, brave and boisterous survivors, probably kept him alive and out on the cricket field for longer than he should. His good fortune in having Alastair Boyd to take over the captain's mantle and all the duties enabled him finally to assume the less taxing role of president.

But what lies beneath all this are some puzzling contradictions. One of his closest friends, Hugh Mackintosh, said there was probably no man of his time who caused as much love and laughter as Squire did. His humour was founded on taking the ridiculous seriously, and in this respect he was like Mr Pickwick, except Mr Pickwick never saw the joke. But Squire's cricketing exploits also appeared short on self-mockery; indeed any merriment at his expense, as Cardus discovered, was not received kindly.

A game might be passing him by, yet people spoke of his leadership qualities. Someone said that he captained his sides 'as Hitler led his armies, not from a study of the textbooks but by the light of poetic intuition', which may explain reports that average cricketers played above themselves and pulled off unlikely victories. Was he really a figure of authority or a control freak? If he had a sharp eye for the follies of human behaviour and frequently exposed them in his work, surely he saw his own follies on the cricket field? Perhaps the joke was that none of his team was ever quite sure of him, which kept them under his thumb. And as time went by, Squire's behaviour at matches became less predictable and less coherent, although he was still determined to show he was in charge. 'One must admit,' says Tatham, 'that some of us were happier when he didn't arrive because the day was easier and the organisation more efficient.'

Even in his working prime, Squire had found the practical side of life a struggle. By 1939, his marriage had collapsed, his debts were out of hand. He was frequently bailed out by friends, often diligent and caring females. Just as he had earlier bailed out so many struggling writers with acts of reckless generosity, he accepted help now without too many qualms.

And he loved his children, was immensely proud of their achievements. He got Raglan and Maurice through his old school, Blundell's, and Anthony through Eton. It was a shattering blow when Maurice, serving in the Fleet Air Arm, was killed in 1943. His daughter, Julia, was married for a while to George Baker, the actor currently best known as 'Inspector Wexford'.

Squire was finally made bankrupt in 1947, which may have brought him some relief; but a further blow came in 1950, when a cottage he rented in Suffolk burnt down. It wasn't the first time he'd lost his possessions. A store containing his pictures, books and letters had been hit by a bomb in 1941. At the time he claimed such things were of no real importance. But now he was homeless and virtually destitute. Shifting about London, he found refuge in a Surbiton hotel run by a friend.

Howarth recalls that though his beard gave him some of the dignity of the grand old man, his dress became increasingly bizarre and shabby. Once at the Athenaeum, 'he was seen wearing white flannels, black evening slippers, a badly moth-eaten, blue, high-necked pullover, a wing collar and an old

Blundellian tie.' But friends stood by him. Macmillan's retained him as one of their advisers; and his book page in the *Illustrated London News* still delivered his quality. He had once been quite a stern critic and sometimes swam against the tide. Of Chekhov's *The Seagull* he wrote:

> But does a soul in the audience mind in the least when Konstantin, the young man, the central figure in the play, shoots himself off stage at the climax of the tragedy? Nobody turns a hair. Nothing has died since nothing has lived. If the whole lot had shot themselves, with the possible exceptions of Nina and the Doctor, we should have been purged with neither pity nor with terror.

Earlier, he had fired this shot at T.S. Eliot when reviewing *The Waste Land* in the *London Mercury* (October 1923):

> I read it several times and am still unable to make head or tail of it. To use Mr Chesterton's emphatic refrain, 'Will someone please take me to a pub?'

He took his son Anthony to task for describing Terence Rattigan as a first-class dramatist ('seems a bit strong for Rattigan'). And he dismissed Noel Coward as 'a gentleman of whom you have probably never heard who writes more or less smart plays in the eighteen-ninety manner'. But his tone softened. In a late review of a book by Somerset Maugham which he obviously disliked, he finished off, 'But what am I doing? Carping? Certainly not.'

He settled finally in the Sussex village of Rushlake Green in a cottage which he shared with a woman friend, Bertha Usborne, and a dog named Bingo which had been found as a stowaway in an aircraft and had somehow attached itself to Squire. In the last months, though virtually bedridden, his

mind remained active, and Miss Usborne, who nursed him devotedly, described him as 'perpetually uncomplaining'.

One could give a rosy glow of all this, but it wouldn't be entirely truthful. There are conflicting stories from friends of uncomfortable visits. Enough to say that the end came peacefully on 20 December 1958. He was 74. He wanted to be buried in Devonshire among his ancestors, but 'fate had one ghoulish malignant trick still in store for him', Howarth records, 'the county boundaries were changed and his grave is today in the county of Cornwall.' Whether Squire would have seen the joke is a moot point.

His legacy...

The kind of lyrical work that Squire championed during and after the First World War was loathed by such as D.H. Lawrence, the Sitwells, T.S. Eliot and Evelyn Waugh. 'Cricket, Belloc, Sussex, walking tours, ballades, punning in pubs' was debunked in the 60s. But whatever judgement is cast on him, that he was a lightweight trundling about in a bygone age, one thing is for sure; his cricketing legacy lives on, and his name will be constantly and affectionately invoked in these pages.

Mike Halliwell's Bistro; pre-season drinks, 2000.

A lively discussion is under way about the influence of alcohol on sport. Someone coins the phrase Alcoholic Synonymous...

...with the Invalids? With any cricket club? Sport in general? It is freely admitted that most need a pint or two to oil the wheels. To the extent that anyone is actually *dependant* on this for their pleasure is a question fairly swiftly ducked. But a day's cricketing without a drink? It is unimaginable. At all levels, watching or playing, sport is a social occasion. And booze invariably produces the best jokes, as seen in the manner that we present Sir John himself.

Someone adds that without alcohol and smoking the British would never have survived, let alone won, two world wars. The fact that this was presumably the same for both sides is glossed over. But a new point emerges. Life, pre-war, for Invalid types in the main was pretty easy-going and leisured, with drinking an accepted part of the culture for both sexes.

Then war accelerated the need and the dependance. And afterwards, knuckling down, raising families, finding jobs in post-war Britain, wasn't a barrel of fun. Some were licking their wounds, literally and metaphorically, some had endured the prison camps; others, for whom service had been long stretches of boredom, followed by a surge of adrenalin, may simply have drunk from the habit of wartime. Whichever camp you fell into, drink brought relief from the drabness and, to hammer the point home, a day in the country with Sir John and his revellers provided the perfect excuse and the outlet.

A sombre moment as glasses are raised in salute to some notable casualties. Then the mood lifts. Booze was the vital connection between the city and the country dwellers, a breaking down of social barriers! It's an upbeat and valid point. As Bill Foss has stated:

> In my day, the Invalids were simply a way of getting out of town, with people one liked. Villages seemed to welcome us because (a) they didn't see people like us very often, and (b) we usually bought the drinks, those of us who stayed. Cricket and alcohol unshackled you and broadened the horizons.

But for a while, maybe, the Invalids took this notion to excess. They drank before, during (from the boot of their motors) and after the game, and wasn't this rather boring? Late arrivals, fumbling displays in the field and generally poor behaviour must frequently have annoyed the home teams ... and this lasted well into the 60s. There were certain occasions when the only contribution an Invalid made to the cricket was to take out a gin and tonic to the square leg umpire.

Nowadays, it's rare to find an Invalid paralytic during or after a game unless he has a driver and no sharp Monday schedule. This isn't down to any kind of moral superiority. Many would love to let rip, but the roads are too busy, the law won't allow it; and on a deeper level, maybe, the modern breed of Invalid carries job and young family responsibilities in a different way from the past; he has been spared the pain and anguish of wars and their aftermath which his father and ancestors endured.

A leap forward in time...

Before picking up on the journey which saw Alastair Boyd take over the reins from Sir John, here is an example of how the Invalids go about their business today.

Sunday, 4 June 2000. Invalids v. Grannies. A long-standing fixture with a fellow wandering side of distinction. It used to be a tough one to get right. The Grannies could turn out some big guns that would blow a sub-standard Invalids apart. Incentive to play? In the past, it was an all-day game with a fabulous lunch and tea on a lovely ground, at Stonegate, deep in the heart of East Sussex. Mention here must be made of the families Pougatch and Villiers-Smith, our genial hosts. Drawbacks? Deep in the heart of East Sussex, roadworks and congestion through Tonbridge and Tunbridge Wells on a weekend. The match manager's perennial panic: would his team arrive on time? He knew they'd arrive in time for lunch, of course. And he has two bad experiences of his own. Once, on the Tonbridge by-pass, carrying three key players, his clutch went. A mile walk back to the nearest phone, long before the days of the mobile, he managed to get Caroline (Mrs Villiers-Smith) provider of the fabulous lunch, to leave her preparations, locate and airlift the three stars to the game.

The match manager then spent a hot Sunday afternoon by his stricken motor, waiting for the AA who finally towed him to a garage in Southborough, where it was left, with a note on the windscreen, on the forecourt. Being a diligent leader of his men, and with nowhere else to go, he hired a taxi to Stonegate. Cost £30. By the time he arrived, having missed the fabulous lunch and tea, he found the Invalids on the point of a rousing win, achieved without him having to change his clothes. A triumph of team selection. And he got a free ride home. On the following Wednesday he was obliged to take time out of his busy schedule to catch a train to Tonbridge, a cab to Southborough, to pick up his car. The whole experience cost him upwards of £500.

Some years later, the same match manager, now living in Swanage, Dorset, got snarled up in traffic and floods in the Southampton area, activated his mobile (which had since been invented) to hear it was clear skies in Stonegate, come on down. He arrived in time to see the winning run hit again by the Invalids. Again he didn't change, and his impressive record against this formidable opposition won him control of the fixture in perpetuity, which brings us to the year 2000.

At the pre-season party, on board Mr Halliwell's floating bistro, the match manager and others in the same boat had reflected complacently on how healthy the club was, how many new talented, personable, young faces had been drawn to the famous old colours, how easy it was to select a side. You scarcely had to lift the phone.

Wednesday 31 May. The match manager counted six players and was waiting on seven or eight fax/email responses which had failed to come back (so much for modern technology). On top of this, the opposing captain, Will Kennerly, was phoning up from Stockport (he was a traveller for W.H. Smith) to say the Stonegate groundsman, a gloomy fellow, was muttering already about the state of the ground. It had, to be fair, been raining all week. Hard to recruit under these conditions; and the lunch inducement had stopped a few years back. Who in their right mind fancied a tedious trip deep into Sussex on a Saturday morning after a stress-filled week? 'Well, if you're really desperate,' became a stock response. On the Thursday afternoon, the match manager scraped in Dave Williams, the partner of his fourth daughter (the Oxford half Blue who refused herself to play, 'No way, dad!'). Dave was honest enough to admit he hadn't played since school (he was now 34), and had no kit. He was selected on the promise he'd be provided with socks, shirt and Invalid sweater if he could just bring some trainers (he was size 12, and there was no-one around with that kind of foot). His trousers were a lesser concern.

Thursday night threw up a bonus. Bill Rodwell, a wily competitor in TV quiz shows and a slow bowler of quizzical guile, announced his availability. He was off to his local and would see if he could pick up a player or two. In the hallowed tradition of Sir John himself, Rodwell had done this before, roping in rugby playing pals and the occasional cricketer to get the Invalids out of a hole. Mike Halliwell, who was recovering from the latest of a series of painful knee operations, announced he was willing to come and umpire. He was immediately selected to play.

Friday 2.30. The Grannies' skipper, now calling from Leicester, said he'd been promised an early pitch inspection by the grumpy groundsman. This never happened. So the match manager set off to stay overnight with one of his players, John Stanley, who lived in Kent. (No chances taken this year with the weather conditions in the Southampton area.) Having arrived safely, and learning that Rodwell had drawn a blank in his London local, recruitments were sought in the village pub.

One to find, hopefully a wicket-keeper/batsman who had his own gear. Stanley spotted someone who'd been a fair cricketer, with decided views on the game, including a strong and unexplained hatred of Bob Woolmer. Within seconds, he revealed himself as a sad and irredeemable alcoholic. Now Stanley had another idea. His friend, John Lawson, a fine veteran cricketer who had agreed to umpire, was pulled out of retirement for one last hurrah, as wicket-keeper and opening batsman. But he had no kit. Two to dress, but a team of sorts assembled. After an excellent supper and a glass or two of wine, the match manager slept easy for the first time in a week and woke to clear skies.

Saturday 12.30. News broke that Charles Symonds-Jones, opening bowler, detailed to bring Rodwell and the bag (scorebook, new ball and wicket-keeping gloves) had been unable to meet up with his second passenger, Ian Hartley, who was marooned the wrong side of Putney Bridge following an IRA bomb scare. Police cordons. No-one allowed across. It had already been established that the actor, Richard Durden, was rehearsing (playing Helen Mirren's husband in *Orpheus Descending* by Tennessee Williams at the Donmar Theatre) and would arrive late.

Four short, without equipment, at least until pushing on teatime, meant the Invalids were obliged to bat first while attempting also to dress two of their players. The match manager stared at the sodden strip that passed for the wicket in dismay. 'We'll bat', he muttered as he won the meaningless toss.

Calling on Squire's gift of bringing the best out of players when the chips were down, the match manager saw the Invalids make a valiant fist of their innings, as re-inforcements dribbled in. One incident stands out: Dave, the partner of the match-manager's daughter, collided in midwicket with Steve Hicks, the leading runmaker, and was run out before he had scored, with his borrowed (but unsupported) box ending up gallantly protecting his right knee-cap. The game went to the wire, where the Grannies scrambled a merited victory. No-one minded that. The match manager went home with a job well done and got on with his life.

Three days later, the Grannies skipper, phoning from Bolton, said that someone had nicked the umpires' coats.

3

DAD'S ARMY

No-one is in any doubt that the Invalids would have sunk, all hands, if Alastair Boyd hadn't stepped in to relieve Sir John of his duties. A big bearded bear of a man, 'pear-shaped', as Foss described him, you might have mistaken him for a Naval commander. He answered cheerfully to the name of 'Buffalo' or more commonly 'Dad'. His daughter Nina points out that this came from her being the only child on the ground in the early days constantly shouting out 'Dad' when requiring attention. The bachelors in the team, Dalmahoy, Foss, Jenkins and Ames, set themselves up as 'The Committee of Uncles.' Their aim was to teach Nina about life. Her parents obviously knew nothing about it, as they had married far too young at the age of 20 and were only 23 when Nina was born.

Alastair was educated at Charterhouse, where he was better known for his squash and his fine treble voice than for his cricket. When the voice broke it was a disaster, but he still sang different parts of operas in the car on the way to and from Invalid matches.

He was studying History at Worcester College, Oxford when war broke out. He volunteered immediately. In North Africa he was wounded in the stomach and spent six weeks in hospital. He recovered well enough not really to qualify as one of Jack Squire's incapacitated Invalids, he always maintained. He was then sent to Italy, where his battalion was so decimated at Anzio that the few survivors, including him, were sent back to the UK. At the end of the war he was a Staff Captain in Ghent. The job was to reintegrate the Belgian troops who had been in the UK under the British Army. One problem he dealt with was the soldier who had his rotten teeth extracted by British Army medics but he was sent back home before they had time to give him his false teeth. The Belgian Army did not feel responsible for this, so in despair the soldier wrote to King George VI, saying, 'The British have taken my teeth whereby I am abandoned.' The letter was passed to Alastair with the instruction that he should do something for the poor man. Quite what he did is not on record.

He met Jack Squire through a group of friends in one of the Ebury Street watering holes. It was 1947, and the Invalids were in poor shape. Alastair pitched in to help and took the radical step of getting a fixture list printed. This was not universally approved, but Squire saw the point and made him vice-captain. By now he was working as a Press Representative for theatre managements; and one hopes that he found persuading a charabanc of tourists into a West End farce easier than getting 11 Invalids to a distant point in the country, roughly on time, with or without a charabanc.

Bill Rodwell gives the following insight on 'Dad'. (Bill, at one time almost part of the Boyd family, refers to himself in the third person)

Physique – Alastair was not a small man. He stood over six feet tall, had a full beard trimmed like George V and an increasing waistline which was sometimes surrounded by a Club tie.

Captaincy – He always captained except for his two weeks holiday in August. When asked what sort of side the Invalids were, he would reply 'Vaguely theatrical'. He loved telling theatre anecdotes. One concerned Clive Barnes, Drama Critic of the *New York Times* and therefore the most powerful man in American theatre, who dismissed the risque *Oh Calcutta!* as 'the sort of show which gives pornography a bad name'.

Team Selection – He discovered that additional bodies, if not actual cricketers, could be fetched up by Bill Rodwell. A telephone call on a Friday afternoon would begin: 'Bill? Alastair here ... I'm three short for Blackboys.' Bill lived next door to the Sun in Splendour in Portobello Road. The pub was the HQ of the Sinners Rugby Football Club where members gathered on Friday evenings. Bill would wait until candidates were sufficiently oiled, then strike. One 'procured' in this way was Tony Joyce, who'd had a few games for Lancashire 2nd XI and was a more than useful cricketer.

Personal – Alastair lived in a flat in Chelsea with the amusing address 'St Loo Mansions, Flood Street'. His family consisted of his wife Betty, who managed a boutique called Spectrum in Gloucester Road and often scored in the early days. Nina was taught this skill when she was nine and carried on the tradition. She met Rodwell at Trinity College, Dublin. He was Best Man at Nina's wedding to a fellow student. The marriage, alas, was a short-lived affair like most (all?) of Bill's innings.

Tatham on Dad...

I felt guilty of the burden we threw on him, but I don't think he wanted it otherwise. As a cricketer, he was a fair all-rounder who batted better each season and bowled worse: comments he took from me with his usual good humour.

Bill Foss adds...

Dad I found charming, a very pleasant fellow, very happy to laugh with you...but he did things his way and wouldn't always take criticism or suggestions, bless his heart! I don't think his professional life was too rewarding. He looked to cricket as his response to life, adored it. The drill was you met at the village pub, had three or four pints and a sandwich, then found your way to the ground. On one occasion, we turned up and there were two teams playing already. Dad had forgotten to confirm the date, so we all had to go home.

When tossing up, he was always guided by what the captain of England was doing at the time. If England were batting, we batted and vice versa. No-one felt inclined to question the logic. Dad was in command: Captain, Secretary, Manager, Selector, Batsman, Bowler. An astute

'Dad's Army'

captain? Not noticeably. You took to the field and waited to see what would happen.

A glance through some early scorebooks reveals:

The Invalids were bowled out regularly for less than 100. Occasionally a strange name would appear with a score of 40 or 50 in a total of 93 all out, but like the sighting of a dolphin off the Dorset coast, he would vanish. An indecent number of second innings were entered half-heartedly in the book, and there were a disturbing number of innings' defeats. These might well include some unfortunate who chalked up scores of 0 and 1 in the space of four and a half hours cricket, having made a round trip of 150 miles – which did wonders for his 'Invalid' average, if nothing else.

On the subject of Dad's driving, David Pritchett remembers:

I was only once or twice a passenger, but he thought he was a Destroyer captain chasing a U-Boat: he would zigzag across the road regularly and get away with it.

Foss adds:

Once, at Peaslake, Dad had just left the pub when he returned, palefaced. Our leader required our services. We hurried out to find his brand new Beetle resting on its side in a ditch. Nina was the driver with Dad in the front instructing and Betty in the back. Nina hadn't yet learnt that you could apply the brake and clutch simultaneously. Dad's response had been, 'I think you got something wrong there.' There was some damage (Betty laddered her stocking), otherwise all was thankfully well. We put our shoulders to the task, half a dozen of us, and in no time we were back in the pub for another pint and much relieved laughter. The spot was afterwards known as 'Nina's Corner'.

Some of the fixtures were decidedly grotty, and one of Alastair's many services to the Invalids were to strike these from the list. In this context, Tatham remembers:

> *Westmill in Hertfordshire* – a piece of more or less undisturbed pastureland, where I first met the 18-year-old Jeremy Paul. I well recall him stepping daintily up to bowl, carefully avoiding the cowpats.
>
> One match went down in the list simply as '*The Plough*'. It was somewhere in Berkshire, though it is difficult to be more specific, and I can't think how we found our way to it. (This could have been where G.K. Chesterton was heading when he sent his famous telegram to his wife – 'Am in Market Harborough, where should I be?')
>
> *Claygate, Hare Lane* – if you went past the ground, you'd have said the area was nearly big enough to play cricket, but not quite. But play they did, on matting, without realising that unless matting was laid on concrete, it was lethal. After Patrick Dalmahoy had been struck by a good length ball which got up and had needed several stitches in his chin, this fixture was discontinued.

Some lost fixtures retained distinctive memories...

Brook, between Godalming and Haslemere, was the scene of the fall of Sir John's trousers. In the days of petrol rationing, it was a difficult place to reach. Once, a party, including Sir

68

John and Mr Mackley, the umpire (who, we may remember, disliked Brook for some reason) found themselves at Witley Station, two miles away. Tatham recalls:

As the youngest present (a mere 35), I was selected to walk to Brook to summon help while the rest settled down to refurbishment in the pub by the station. It was a hot day. When I reached the ground, I received little sympathy, it being pointed out that there were such things as telephones, which I suppose was fair comment.

We played several times on the excellent *West Herts* ground at Watford against the *Handlebar Club* (President Raymond Glendenning: Vice President Jimmy Edwards), an amiable and rather extrovert collection who sported handlebar moustaches. They were not very good cricketers, but on one occasion, they included one who was distinctly above the Handlebar average. At the end of the game he removed his moustache and was revealed as a certain Tony Reynolds. Alastair promptly signed him on for the Invalids, for whom he played for several years before taking off for Africa.

Simon Collins adds this about Reynolds...

In 1986, I was a committee member of the East India Sports Club. A friend at this time was an ex-Hurricane fighter pilot of the Second World War, Tony Reynolds. One day, he saw me sporting the Invalids tie and all but fell off his chair. He produced a faded photograph of himself circa 1947 (clean shaven), and next to him ... Boris Karloff? His friend and guest, no less! I wish now that I had a copy of this priceless photograph: the day that Boris Karloff played for the Invalids.

Dad and Boris Karloff reaching for the stars

More lost fixtures...

Chiddingfold was a good place to play but it had one oddity. The sight-screen, opposite the pavilion was fixed, apparently immovably, to the same tree, so that only occasionally, by chance, did it serve any useful purpose.

The Invalids have since shifted to a country house game at Follies Farm (Old Spots), but the Chiddingfold Inn still retains pre-match Invalids custom.

Peaslake **once hosted the final match of the season. Tatham relates:**

It will have been noted the Invalids were no novice beer drinkers, but it always seemed that more was consumed at the Windmill Inn, Peaslake than anywhere else. Confirmation of this came on the night Patrick Dalmahoy's car went missing. It was discovered next morning round the corner, driven there by some skylarking lads and left. When Patrick went back to get it, the landlord said he was pleased the Invalids were coming back next year, because on the previous Sunday evening, he had sold 120 pints of beer.

Once at Peaslake, Ray Harrison was fielding at mid-off. Usually he had a safe pair of hands, as befitted a member of the Harlequins first XV. This time, however, he dropped a dolly catch. Moments later, he caught an absolute snorter in the same position, just as the umpire bellowed 'No-ball.'

Sadly the Peaslake fixture bit the dust. Dad received the following letter, dated 8 April (mid 1950s).

Dear Mr Boyd,

I regret to say that after many years we are forced to give up cricket in Peaslake, and I have to cancell [*sic*] all fixtures. I apologise for the short notice and hope you will find a replacement.

Yours sincerely

J.E. Richardson (Match sec. Hazelbrow Poultry Farm, Rad lane, Peaslake)

On the back of this letter is scribbled the cryptic message 'Gone to Brenda's.'

A fixture list for 1953 reveals that of 16 games listed, only one, **Penshurst**, remains today. But some have come and gone and returned. In particular, **Rodmell**, believed to be Sir John's favourite. In the late 1950s they were skippered by the actor William Fox who, with his actress wife Patricia Hilliard, laid on after-match parties in his cottage for 'any who didn't have to rush away.' No-one, as far as is known, rushed away, and Fox and Boyd exchanged a lively and quixotic correspondence when trying to shore up next year's fixtures. Example: from Fox to Boyd, 16 February 1956.

Please don't think me too awful for not answering your first letter last autumn. Our secretary was taken seriously ill and all our fixtures got lost somewhere in his cottage. He died last month. But we'd very much like you to visit if August 12 is still free. The Invalids fixture is becoming very popular with the village and we look forward to seeing you in time for a 2.30 start. Don't bother to confirm.

The 2.30 start would have been optimistic. From Fox to Boyd a year later answering an invitation to the Invalids winter dinner...

I have delayed answering until my plans were certain and alas! I have to play in a *Saturday Night Theatre* on the BBC that evening. Unfortunately it is live and not recorded as I'd hoped. Pat and I are very disappointed and hope we may be invited again next year. All good wishes from us both. Bill.

Apart from having a distinguished career in the theatre, Fox served with the London Irish Rifles (1939–45) at home and abroad, reaching the rank of Major. He helped found the Reunion Theatre Association for demobilised artists.

The Blackboys connection was made at this time. A letter from Mr Nicholls, their secretary, dated 18 July 1957, reads as follows:

72

Dear Mr Boyd ... we shall never forget the marvellous game we had, and the village could not have had a better for the first ever Sunday match at Blackboys. We really did not deserve to win after your 'generosity', but the result, of course, did not matter. With very best wishes...

This would seem to be the first written record of the Invalids snatching defeat from the jaws of victory, but it was arguably a PR exercise and the fixture is happily flourishing today.

One of the pleasant duties which befalls the Invalids, introduced by Alastair around this time, is to chip in with donations whenever a village needs to improve their amenities: in gratitude for all the favours we receive, year in, year out. To give an example, here is a letter which has caught the eye:

From: Tichborne Park, Nr Alresford, Hants, 28 March 1955
To: The Secretary of the Invalids Cricket Club.

Dear 'Sir' (a round-robin letter)
The Tichborne Park Cricket Club has never in the course of its existence over 100 years possessed a pavilion, although the matter has been discussed on many occasions. Up to date we have relied on a marquee, but this has proved very costly and our present marquee is well beyond repair. It is felt that the moment has now come to have a permanent building on the ground, and it is for this reason that I am writing to you.

You will realise of course that the cost of such a building is beyond the resources of a club as small as we are, but it is hoped that between the members and the many friends which I believe the club has, we will be able to raise the necessary sum.

Expert advice informs us that this sum will be in the region of £600: this may seem a large amount, but we feel strongly that a building must be erected that is both worthy of the ground and of such a nature that it will not collapse at the first puff of wind!

If you can see your way to helping us by even the smallest of donations we would be more than grateful and you would be helping to further the cause of a club which, although small, has, I am convinced, done its share in promoting the welfare of cricket in this county.

I thank you in anticipation,

> Yours truly,
> Sir Anthony Tichborne, Bart, President.

Any donations should be sent etc etc...

As begging letters go, the above is as good as you get, and it is certain that the Invalids responded (the sum unknown).

Norman Neale chips in with a 'Dad' story...

We were playing at Burleigh, two players short when Alastair noticed two young soldiers in uniform watching from the boundary. So he asked them to play and they cheerfully agreed. Without getting out of their uniform, one of them bowled the home side out, and the other knocked off the runs while the rest of us watched in awe. The infuriated opposition promptly dropped the Invalids from their fixture list.

James Lipscombe (no mean performer in the era of drought) intriguingly provides another 'soldier' story which, given the capricious nature of memory (on which these pages

'Without getting out of their uniform'

thrive), may just be the same event as the above, mashed into one.

I'll tell the tale. It was about 1960 or words to that effect, I was playing for the Invalids all that summer with David Pritchett and Ray Harrison and some other great guys and the essence of it was, I was also serving with 21 SAS …

and we were on weekend exercise ... and as we were
passing through the Limpsfield area where Ray lived, we
stopped and met Ray in the pub who said, 'We're playing at Hawkhurst tomorrow and we're very short.' So
anyway we went on down and finished the exercise down
at the old shooting range at Hythe ... and I said to the
Sqron S'arnt Major, 'If you're doing nothing this afternoon, would you like to play cricket?' To which he said,
'That's a good idea, that's what we'll do.' And so we all
turned up in army boots and the whole thing ... and we
made up half the side. They batted first and the guys took
this all in great humour and the Sarn't Major didn't get
very many runs, two or three, and was sitting on the steps
of the pavilion looking at his bat, and those days they had
little oiling instructions on the back and he said, 'Ah, I
know what's wrong, I didn't read the instructions!'

Neale again...

Another time, at Blackboys where the famous comedy
actor Ronald Shiner owned the local inn, the actress Dora
Bryan was visiting with her husband, Bill Lawton. Both
teams were one short, and Alastair generously offered
Bill to the locals while accepting an 11-year-old boy for
the Invalids. Unfortunately nobody had told Alastair that
Lawton played cricket for a living and we were back in
the pub before opening time.

SIR JOHN'S FRIENDS
(*Evening Standard*, Londoner's Diary, Saturday
19 April 1969)
The Invalids Cricket Club, one of the oldest and most
famous touring sides in the South of England, last night
celebrated their 50th anniversary in the suitable sur-

roundings of the MCC committee room in the pavilion at Lord's. The club was founded by Sir John Squire whose only stipulation for membership was 'that they may be a friend of mine'.

He evidently did not confine his athletic friends to those who played cricket. On one occasion he took a side to play a village in Sussex, boasting that he had 'seven Blues in the eleven'. The village was somewhat surprised at the ease with which they defeated the Invalids – until the genial Jack Squire confessed that not one had a Blue for cricket.

The event described was the culmination of a flurry of debate and activity among the hierarchy on how the Invalids should best parade their history, their existence, their survival. Some wondered if the choice of Lord's as venue wasn't a shade presumptuous. On cricketing efforts alone, the Invalids could scarcely claim a footprint in the margins of the game. And yet? Lord's was booked, invitations despatched to all and sundry (each village sending a representative) and the menu for the record was *Egg in Aspic*, *Fillet of Sole Chauchart*, *Boeuf Bourgignonne*, *Croquette Potatoes*, *Brussels Sprouts*, *Carrots Vichy* ... and *Savoury Invalids*. The wine was *Chablis 1967*, *Chateau Beau Rouge 1961* and *Martiez 1955*.

There were two regrettable absentees. Raglan Squire had architectural commitments in Cyprus but sent a message which echoed his father's words years before. *'So sorry not to be with you. Best wishes to the Invalids on their 50th birthday and here's to the next 50 years. Rag Squire.'*

And Edmund Blunden wrote two letters, the first on 6 March:

My dear Alastair,

The season is already hurrying on ... and it is splendid of you to have kept Jack Squire's joyous invention alive so long. May this new season be as merry as any earlier one. I am much honoured by your invitation to me to be President of the Club, though I must be forgiven for all feebleness – so different from Jack and his 'all the talents'. And at 72 years old I really am a shadow. If I do not manage the dinner on 18 April, I beg to be forgiven – even our small car is usurped by one or other of the young. But I shall try gratefully to take the chance of what will be a joyous occasion.

Best wishes to Betty, you and all,
Yours ever, Edmund.

A letter written on the same day by his wife Claire to Alastair indicates that Blunden was putting up a gallant struggle of mind over matter...

I think it is *most* unlikely that Edmund will be able to manage the dinner ... much as he would like to be at Lords that evening. His health is not at all good ... he worries terribly about any engagement which tires him ... especially if it involves meeting a number of people... I am sorry about this but the doctor's advice has to be taken...

Or were they being over-protective? A letter from our President on 16 April in much firmer handwriting...

My dear Alastair,

If the years would be kinder I should make a bolder effort to share what will be a joyous evening, and how wonderful if Jack Squire opened with one of his laughing speeches. It is a great thing that so large a company will be gathering and preludes I am sure all the triumphs as well as the excitements of the season. I am deeply honoured, unworthy though I am, at being made President.

With greetings to Invalids all and the assurance from some mysterious spirit that all will flourish splendidly game after game... Affectionately, Edmund.

Edmund Blunden won the MC, and his book *Undertones of War*, published in 1928, was widely recognised as the best statement of the experiences of front-line troops in the First World War. He was awarded the Hawthornden Prize for literature at the age of 26 and was Professor of Poetry at Oxford

Edmund Blunden and Sir John

(1966–68). Concerning cricket, he claimed consideration 'as a wicket-keeper who has taken seven wickets in an innings out of nine altogether.' A much respected and much loved man, he died in 1974.

The night the Invalids came to Lord's was voted an unqualified success, and when a pedant pointed out that the celebration was one year too soon (the first match having taken place in 1920), he was quickly silenced. This was an 'Invalid' centenary, i.e one short of a hundred.

Alastair in his speech of welcome had this to say about Jack Squire...

Many of us knew him as a man of enormous charm. He had many distinctions, as a poet, editor, critic, conversationalist and as the only cricket captain to arrive at matches 40 or 50 miles outside London in a London taxi. He would emerge already dressed in his white flannels, while the taxi driver, Len, would change more prosaically in the pavilion and come out to keep wicket, which he did very well.

Jack Squire was never a great cricketer ... but his enthusiasm for the game was colossal and infectious ... and as a recruiter of teams he was a genius. On a Thursday evening he would have himself and no-one else, but by the weekend he would have collected 8, 9 or 15 players – never 11. He had a boyish sense of humour which prompted him, on one occasion, to try and raise a side of players with names that corresponded with those of well-known firms, as it were, Marks, Spencer, Mappin, Webb, Freeman, Hardy and Willis, and what's more he nearly succeeded.

Alastair then speaks warmly of the new President, Professor Blunden, and calls on the distinguished author, Laurence Meynell, who played between the wars and attended many of the famous dinners at the Cheshire Cheese in Fleet Street, to propose the toast of the Club. Alec Reid, who 'has always been one of our best fielders with a style of his own, tackling every ball that comes his way as if it were a front row forward' proposed the health of the guests. And Herbert Hunter from Penshurst, 'a worthy and much respected opponent for many years who knows us well,' replied for the guests.

On 29 April, a gracious thank-you letter with a sad coda arrived at the Boyd house.

Dear Alastair,

What a magnificent evening ... I had never dined at Lord's before and much appreciated hanging my coat in the players' dressing room.

I regret to say that the Torry Hill Club is not able to entertain you in return this year because we simply have not got our ground ready or our players organised. Our leading action-man moved out of the district ... and we have missed his lead so much that we will have to scratch next Sunday's game ... it goes against the grain telling you this in a letter thanking you and the Invalids for your wonderful hospitality. I can only emphasise my apologies ... and hope that next year Torry Hill CC will rise to the occasion a bit better.

Yours, Robin Leigh Pemberton.

The writer was to become Governor of the Bank of England, but the fixture with Torry Hill CC survived only briefly.

Continuing our journey, Richard Butler, now the Club's treasurer, recalls his first game...

It was the summer of 1970. The Americans, the year before, had put a man on the moon and England had a good Test side. I had decided that I didn't want to play cricket in a London League and mentioned this one day to Bill Rodwell, who told me of the famous wandering club he belonged to. 'Come and play for us,' he suggested, 'we're often a bit short.' In fact it seemed they were five short for the coming Saturday. As it was then Thursday, this historic club was obviously able to waive any of the vetting/nets/application form requirements that had been the rule at my previous club, and I was asked to ring one Alastair Boyd as soon as possible to volunteer my services. Alastair eagerly gave me directions to a public house in Kent – something about going up a hill out of Sevenoaks, turning left at a broken signpost then driving through a wood. (The sign actually remained broken for a further ten seasons and continued to serve as an excellent pointer for new players to the Underriver match. Invalid directions, I was to learn, would always concentrate on essentials. 'Cowden? Down the A22 and left at the Wing Wah Chinese restaurant.')

I found the sign, meandered through the woods and into an idyllic village where I duly landed at the White Rock Inn. I looked around for cricketers I had been assured would be there, but saw no-one that bore the slightest resemblance to the young athletes I had been playing with at Barnes. There was a group of largely elderly gentlemen, drinking gin and laughing loudly, led by a splendid character with a red and white spotted handkerchief round his neck, addressing everyone as 'dear boy', and it was he who established contact with the diffident recruit.

82

Some time well after 2.30 the group left the pub and proceeded to a cricket ground, surrounded by cornfields. My memories of the actual game are hazy now, but one or two things come back with considerable clarity. The opposition batted first and I remember the almost complete lack of any attempt at fielding on the part of the Invalids. Here, clearly, was a strong batting side who needed a large total to go for. The up-and-down military bowling, employed at both ends for the entire innings, was also consistent with this assessment. I remember taking a straightforward catch in the deep, which was greeted as something altogether remarkable and rewarded with great acclaim.

Tea was sensational and prolonged. Then we batted and I was sent out to umpire. Underriver had a wicket-keeper called Aeneas Perkins. We had an imposing opening bat who had been described to me as a 'poker player', who fairly soon was palpably leg before to a perfectly straight ball. Loud appeal – absolutely plumb. I was just raising my finger when the poker player snorted 'What – from left arm round?' and glared contemptuously down the wicket at me and the bowler. Even today I curl up in shame when I remember my cowardice. I feebly muttered 'Not out' and made an unconvincing attempt to scratch my nose with the offending finger.

A latter-day Bobby Southcott, a young man in a navy blue pullover called Speedy, then made an elegant 90, giggling every time he hit the ball, and the Invalids reached a reasonable total. I batted low down and made 13. I don't remember who won. There was a wonderful evening in the White Rock, and great insistence that I play the following week at Fernhurst, where I was promoted to Number 4. In fact I played every game for the rest of that season, and didn't miss many in the next 30 years.

John Shepherd offers this titbit on his first and (almost only) game) before he found his comfortable niche for a number of seasons as 1st XI scorer, from which position he had a privileged and unbiased view of life.

Bill Rodwell and I were homeless at one time, so we went to Alastair's house and borrowed his tent. He was a camping type of person, a very calm man, the adversity of being eight short didn't seem to upset him. I think that's how I got to play a couple of times although you couldn't dignify it with the word 'play...'

I remember the worst pub we ever went to. It was at Holyport. We came in and saw this old crone playing a piano in her sitting room. She didn't take any notice, so we went 'knock, knock'. She looked at us furiously. 'Yes?' 'Two pints of your excellent bitter, please.' She brought us two pints of what looked and tasted like paint stripping fluid. I asked Alastair why we met here when there seemed to be a perfectly good pub over the road. 'I got short-changed there ten years ago,' he said. 'Never been back.'

Dear Mr Bladderwick (ran the letter), it is very kind of you indeed to lend us your cricket ground once again this year for our Old v. New Invalids match, on Sunday, July 20th. We look forward to as good a day as we had last year and we hope that you will be with us. Margaret Foss has told me that Mrs Bladderwick might be able to make some arrangements about tea and we would appreciate this. Would you let me know if this can be done and what the charge per head would be? Could we also have the use of your stumps and balls?
  Yours Sincerely,
    Alastair Boyd
    Captain & Hon Secretary,
    The Invalids.

This letter was written on 26 June 1969 and is a perfect example of three things about Dad. His charm, his resourcefulness and the sheer bloody hard work it takes to run the Invalids!

Alastair died suddenly just after the end of the 1970 season. Bill Rodwell records how it happened.

Alastair played squash very well for a big man. He was able to dominate inferior opponents by standing on the 'T' and dictating matters from there. He played regularly at Dolphin Square on a Saturday morning, took a swim in the pool, then repaired to the George IV pub where he would find a gathering of Invalids. One Saturday, he played as usual but felt a little strange in the changing room afterwards. His GP recommended that he didn't play the following week but, if he felt up to it, he should be OK to play in a fortnight, which he did. This time, he had a massive heart attack and died a few days later in hospital. He was 50.

R.I.P. (Revered Invalid Personality).

For those of us playing at this time, Alastair <u>was</u> the Invalids. He'd recruited a great number of us, shifting the emphasis away from the cliques of pre-war literary types and post-war cronies, and had put together a family, a rag-bag of disparate characters, forging close and often unlikely friendships which last to this day. What an achievement! And it may be that he left at the right moment. It was becoming harder than ever to run the club single-handed, and could he ever have adjusted to the delegation of duties that was now being demanded? It's doubtful. But he saw us through a transition which at times was by no means easy.

Dad

4

'PRITCH'

One of the mysteries of the Invalids is how a new Captain comes into being. There is no puff of white smoke from the Vatican (or any hostelry of a similar name). There is no discernible hand of democracy, nor has one ever been aware of keen rivalry for the job. Apparently, it's in the gift of the outgoing Captain to name his successor. The very opposite of democracy, you might say, but there has never yet been a murmur of complaint.

David Pritchett was Alastair's right and obvious choice. Hereafter known as Pritch, he was educated at Sherborne, where he was a fine batsman and a useful change bowler. After serving in the Army, he spent some time in the East as a tea broker and returned to London to work in Commodities. He played mainly for 'The Stragglers of Asia' before graduating 'down' to the Invalids, though he would disdain such a term. He was part of a surge of new faces which included Ray Harrison, David Rees, Robin Langrishe, Jeremy Paul and Julian Belfrage, the theatrical agent for the cream of English acting talent, some of whom were, on dire occasions, pressed into service as Invalid cricketers.

Shortly after came Leo Cooper, Tim Jaques, John Divett, Daryl Cantor, Bill Rodwell, Richard and Clive Butler, Mike Halliwell, Matthew Walters, Jeremy Kemp, John Timbers and John Lund. To give names, of course, risks offence to those omitted, but the point is that Alastair did finally have some talent at his disposal – even as, in the honourable tradition of the Invalids, results didn't necessarily reflect it.

Like both his predecessors, there would be no Invalids today without Pritch's management skills and dedication. If his style seemed on occasions, to some of his more laid-back brethren, autocratic (something he himself freely admits), it was essential for the team and the times he inherited.

A conversation between David Pritchett and Jeremy Paul over a convivial lunch at Pritch's house sets the tone for the new regime.

DP: It was Bill Foss and Pat Dalmahoy who very much supported me when Alastair died so suddenly. After that memorable game at Outwood, the last game of the season, where you took six wickets.

JP: Oh yes, I bowled out of the dipping sun and nobody could see the thing...

DP: That's it, you came out of the trees ... and John Lund and I put on what may still be a record, 150 for the first wicket, and Lund went on, much to everyone's annoyance and made 100, he did try and get out but, yes ... that was Alastair's last game.

JP: Describe Alastair.

DP: Well, he was a quiet person, a very nice person, I liked him very much, and he put up with a hell of a lot. There was a form of civil war going on for several years, with Harrison and the Unilever lot on one side and the sort of Hooray Henry lot, shall we say, with Langrishe, Belfrage and myself – Lund never knew quite where he was...

JP: Bill Foss said this was when some of the older ones eased off. The new faces seemed to have money or were very relaxed about the lack of it ... and talked a lot about Annabels, and Claridges and fast motors.

'Out of the dipping sun'

DP: Well, the older ones had money too ... many of them were executive-style people.

JP: But they worked hard for it. The word Foss used for the new intake was 'effete'.

DP: Did he now? Well, I wasn't aware that anyone had ever called me effete. He was probably referring to someone like Robin Langrishe. I mean, Robin was a very generous chap, he would always buy drinks when it was his turn. But there was an occasion ... we had two games over a weekend, we were staying at the Harrisons or roundabout and they had a party. On the Sunday morning, Robin went into the local pub and cashed a cheque to buy Harrison a drink, and unfortunately it bounced. No question of it bouncing forever because there was money behind Robin, he just was always in a chaotic state. Anyway the publican told Ray Harrison, who blew his top, made a great case of it which we thought was very poor, and so for the rest of that season and the whole of the next, we would not drink in the pub afterwards, we'd shove off. So poor old Alastair had this...

JP: ... divided dressing room.

DP: Yes, and dressing rooms in our sort of cricket can be short on space.

JP: What did Alastair do? Did he use diplomacy?

DP: No, I don't think he was a diplomat, really at all. He was quite stubborn, quite firm of purpose. Of course, when he ran the Invalids it was his life. I'm quite sure it wasn't my life, I was keen on it, but I felt we should have match managers and become more like a proper club. It was a bit shambolic to begin with because, I mean, when a chap like John Divett was match manager, you had to do all the work for him.

JP: The Charterhouse incident?

DP: Yes ... well, John and I were having a non-speakers at that time. I'd been in and out of rows with him over the years and this was a bad one, it was very unfortunate. The game against the Sporting Club of Lisbon I'd arranged with this chap Dawson (I'd met him out there playing for one of Bertie Joel's strange teams).

To interrupt for a moment...

Bertie Joel will need no introduction to anyone reading this book. On one of (many) memorable Joel performances, your guide recalls him running The Stragglers game against the Royal Household in Windsor Great Park. Bertie at an advanced age, batting 11, two to win in the last over, with a 'proper' batsman screaming for the strike, blocked out six balls with utter aplomb and explained in the bar afterwards that he didn't do the running any more, but he wasn't giving up his wicket or his cricket. Shades of Sir John Squire.

What Bertie will be remembered for, often in hand with Bill Franklyn, is the thousands of pounds he raised with his 'strange teams' for charity.

Resuming Pritch and the Charterhouse saga...

DP: So the Lisbon side came over and I'd told John he could run the game. He did something very odd with the batting order, I batted 10 ... the whole thing was a shambles.

John Divett (known as 'Speedy' for his lethal deliveries, on and off the field) gives his side of the story.

As an old boy, I was able to arrange the game on the school Third XI ground. In recognition, I was entrusted with the captaincy. I fielded a good side and felt the order of the batting would make little difference to the result. I had at the time a young girlfriend of 18. I put all the names in a hat and asked her to pull them out. It so happened that I went in 11 and Pritchett 10. The match was a closely fought contest, and in the tradition of the Invalids we managed to lose. The captain of the Portuguese side had a wife living nearby and she asked us back to a party. All I can recall of it was going upstairs to chat up the Portuguese au-pair and being told by Pritchett to behave myself! Later I remember talking to the mother and thinking, can I get through this without throwing up? I went outside for fresh air and spent the next few hours lying in a cabbage patch.

I came round to hear people bidding farewells, and staggered to the door to thank our hostess for a lovely evening. I then took my girlfriend, Susie, to the Lake Hotel in Godalming, where Julian Belfrage, Robin Langrishe and Jeremy Kemp were staying. The hotel was locked up so I climbed the fire escape and managed to gain entry. The rest of the evening is a blur, but when we

'Spent the next few hours in a cabbage patch'

came down to breakfast Jeremy, in good form, introduced us all as celebrity actors. The waitress recognised Jeremy and treated the rest of us with open-mouthed awe.

Speedy, for the record, played for Charterhouse in 1948 and in the same year had a trial for Hampshire. He opened the batting for Kenya against the Combined Services in 1953 and bowled first change. Modestly, he continues:

Subsequently not much to shout about, but I looked on Invalid cricket as more of a social event than serious cricket – and no place for prima donnas.

John Timbers and Jeremy Kemp give an impartial eye-witness account of the Charterhouse affair to Jeremy Paul over lunch at the Chelsea Arts Club.

JT: ... it was a lovely day. They batted first and got whatever, one of those afternoon scores which was neither ridiculous or...
JK: 160 ... 170?
JT: ... and Speedy, who was probably being replenished by Langrishe's gin bar out of the back of his Bentley, said, 'Let's draw the names out of a hat for the batting order ... well, Sod's Law immediately rules that...'
JK: Pritch came out last.
JT: ... and he gave a wonderful imitation of Mr Toad.
JK: Didn't speak to Speedy for a year?
JP: That's right, and they'd shared a flat together! When they first met, Pritch asked him if he played cricket. Speedy said, 'Actually I played for Kenya.' 'Oh?' said Pritch. 'Well, you'd better come and play for the Invalids.'
JK: Did he find himself out of his depth?

JP: Well, the first ball he ever bowled for the Invalids bounced halfway down the pitch and flew over the wicket keeper's head, one bounce, four byes.

JK: After that Charterhouse game ... there was astonishing hospitality provided by friends of the Lisbon Sporting Club. We were in somebody's house.

JT: I went home ... I was quite heavily involved with Belinda at that time (now Mrs Timbers) and was playing against Blackboys the next day. Belinda came and couldn't believe her eyes. Half the team from the day before weren't speaking!

JK: So you missed Speedy spread-eagled on his E-type?

JT: On the bonnet?

JK: ... refusing to move, but insisting he was perfectly all right to drive. Julian, Robin and myself, we'd booked rooms in some hotel. Julian and Robin were sharing and I was to be in a single. Well, after Speedy's performance it was quite apparent he had to go in the single and we bunked up, the three of us... I remember a terrifying descent from the party, Speedy driving the E-type down a steep hill ... we were clearly less intoxicated (than Speedy), that's for sure ... and it was very late too.

JP: What year...?

The match was played on 14 August 1971. Sporting Club batted first and scored 154-7. The Invalids replied with 140 all out. For the record, those involved in this story fared thus: Timbers (opening) made 2. Paul (number 3) made 1. Belfrage (number 8) made 0. Kemp (number 9) was lbw Hasslacher 19, Pritchett (number 10) was bowled Williams 19, and Divett (number 11) was not out 0.

The following day at Blackboys, the home side made 177-8, with Timbers, in front of his future wife, bowling 17 overs, 1 maiden, and taking 2-59. Paul bowled 2 overs for 22 and was taken off sharply. Divett bowled 3 overs for 19 and was also removed. In the Invalids reply, Pritch, opening with

Kemp, made 36, including 6 fours and a 6. Kemp was bowled Alcock 29. Divett, batting 3, was run out for 11, in a partnership of some interest (21) with his captain – a Silent Order? Paul (number 4) made 7 and Belfrage (number 7) made 0. Match drawn.

It might seem curious to record these obfuscated details at such length, but they carry an odd kind of fascination.

Lunch with Pritch and Paul resuming...

DP: So that was the end of the Charterhouse affair. It shouldn't have been as bad as that, but it took off, gradually, the idea of match managers... Julian Belfrage managed one or two. His White Waltham game was very much his own business. He knew the Cornwells (John Le Carré's family) who lived thereabouts.

JP: I remember. Godfrey Evans played for them, or was it for us? Godfrey jovially bounced my daughter Sophie on his knee (she was later the Oxford half Blue for cricket). I carry the image of it with an absolute thrill.

DP: Well, I imagine you would.

JP: Belfrage's picnics, highly organised, with quail's eggs a delicacy.

DP: And the Belfrage boys, Rupert and Crispian in short trousers, amused themselves by stuffing everyone's car exhausts with newly cut grass.

JP: We had a pretty healthy fixture list when you took over?

DP: Yes, and I'm delighted to see we still have practically all of them... Blackboys, Rodmell, Penshurst and Underriver, Balcombe ... still very solidly with us... Nettlebed...

JP: We've lost one or two. The Worcester College Rustics...

DP: Yes, Alastair's old college. That was a pity, a lovely place to play. I was sorry to see that go.

The Rustics were not the college team. They were an alternative bunch of undergrads who often included an American Olympic oarsman sampling his first taste of the game. It was an early-season fixture and a good time to get a few runs or wickets under your belt to give you quiet confidence for the sterner tests ahead. It wasn't until after the fixture was discontinued that the Invalids learnt that built into the Rustics' club manifesto was that they must, on no account, ever win a game.

JP: We famously lost Ockley, didn't we, out of some behavioural...?

DP: Now that one Julian was running ... and this particular year no-one wanted to play, so poor Julian had to turn up with a side...

JP: Lot of actors ... John Hurt played...?

DP: ... and we were all out for 23. Did you play? Tony Hobbs was one of us and he lived in the village. He was appalled at how badly we played.

Some confusion here. The records show Invalids all out for 14 against Ockley in 1971, the week before the Charterhouse game. No Tony Hobbs, no John Hurt, but Edward Hardwicke (later Dr Watson to Jeremy Brett's Sherlock Holmes in Granada's TV series) was bowled Brabon K., 1.

DP: Do help yourself to a bit of paté ... that is duck paté and that is some French country job...

At this moment the two lunches merge. As JP helps himself to some excellent paté, we switch back to Timbers and Kemp at the Chelsea Arts Club for an attempted clarification of the Ockley fiasco (or series of fiascos).

JT: ... Belfrage was match manager, he'd got a feeble side and

Tony Hobbs said to him, after someone had bowled a couple of quite dreadful overs, 'If you give that man another over, I'm going home.' Julian promptly gave him another over, and Hobbs went home, leaving his bat behind. The team all signed it and posted it to him. And this is the preamble to me becoming match-manager, knowing we'd been slaughtered the previous year. I did get one or two ringers in, Martin Mather ... Jilly Cooper was there, I remember, Leo was playing...

JP: Didn't they put out their Second XI?

JT: No, they didn't. I won the toss and said, 'We'll bat'. The Ockley skipper went white and said, 'Are you sure?' I told him not to worry, we'd got different personnel this year. 'Well, if you want it over by tea,' he said. I thought, you...! Anyway we batted, Mather made 60, Leo and others made runs ... by ten to 5 we'd got 240 and I declared. Early tea. They came out with a man wearing a Surrey Second XI sweater, quickly spotted by those who recognise these things. He scored a very uncultured 40 in an hour and a half. Killed the game stone dead. At ten past 7 they were something like 120 for 3.

JK: What fun.

JT: Belfrage was playing, so I said, 'Come on, toss a few in the air, they can't possibly score over a 100 in 20 minutes.' He proceeded to take 5 for 25. They finished up about 170 for 8 or 9. And dropped us.

JK: On what grounds?

JT: On the grounds that they couldn't work us out. They were bewildered.

JP: I'm sure there was an Ockley story when David Warner and John Hurt played in some sort of cock-up.

JK: They did. Warner was down in the scorebook as 'A Tall Man', and Hurt...

JP: Retired Hurt?

JK: A.N. Other.

Another game at Ockley...

Invalids fielding, two short. Down the country road that skirts the ground comes a car loaded with luggage and pulls up sharply. The occupants have recognised the fielder by the square leg fence as their school captain of cricket, ten years previously. Bill Minns is that night emigrating to Australia and his friend, David Evans, is driving him to Heathrow. As Providence would have it, they've taken the scenic route with time in hand, and before they know what's happening, both are in borrowed gear and playing. Minns hits an unbeaten 50, gets back in the car and heads off into the sunset.

Thirty years later, on a fleeting return to England, Minns meets up, by curious chance, his old school captain (your guide through these pages). His success in life Down Under, he says, was kick-started by a dream he had of his last day in England. The sun shone gloriously, he was playing cricket God knows where, in borrowed kit. '*You* were playing,' he says. 'Not a dream,' says I, 'you're in the book.'

A medley of memories...

JP: There are times where the memory goes completely AWOL. I found in an old scorebook a match when I scored 68 out of about 101 all out and took eight wickets. I have no recollection of this...

JT: Well you wouldn't, would you!

JP: Yes, but surely something would have stuck.

JK: I hit a six in the Charterhouse game, the only one I ever hit in my life, I know that.

JT: On the school ground? Good Lord, it's huge!

JP: It's true. I've got the scorebook to prove it.

JT: At Holyport once, they'd scored 240. Not a lot to chase on a small ground, as long as you don't waste time fetching the ball out of the river, it's fine. I think we'd lost 3 for 20. Then Matthew Walters and I came together and we put on something like 170 in an hour and ... well, we'd done all the hard work, no need to panic, but we nearly threw it away, finished up just winning by two wickets. I made about 60.

JP: No, you made 80.

JT: Did I? Well, this was in the old days when there were wonderful village characters who batted without gloves ... they were gobsmacked that we got the runs, because it was their highest score for years; they said in the pub, 'Well I don't know, you fellows, it don't seem to matter how many we score, you reckon you're going to get 'em.' And I said, well it <u>was</u> one of our better days.

JK: In the Alastair years I recall confidence was pretty low.

JP: Yes, in the late 50s, the Alastair years were, in terms of results, for the most part, awful, endless collapses...

JT: I remember my first bowl for Alastair...

JK: Where was that, guv?

JT: Balcombe. At the pavilion end ... which if you're trying to bowl leg breaks...

JK: Not clever...

JT: Particularly if the wicket's on the edge of the square sloping down to the wood.

JK: Very good for blackberries, that wood.

JT: Yes, but this was in May. And after bowling three overs with me tweaking the ball like mad and nothing happening, I suggested to Alastair I might be on at the wrong end, and he said, 'Well you'd better come off.' I didn't get another bowl until August!

Back with Pritch, memories of Dad...

DP: At Holmbury St Mary, was it? They had a captain. They

99

both had identical beards and they didn't get on at all. I got into trouble there once, I said to Alastair, look, you must let some other chaps have a bat. Every time I played I'd open, usually with John Lund. It was wonderful, you built up a rapport, but this day I persuaded Alastair we should bat 9 or 10, let others have a go. And sure enough, in true Invalids fashion, we're 50 for 7 and he looked at me sort of reproachfully, so I never ventured that idea again.

JP: Fair to say that Alastair sometimes rather hogged the batting and the bowling?

DP: Yes, but he wasn't such a bad player, you know...

JP: He made 94 against Outward...

DP: And he was quite quick, he took wickets.

JP: Plenty.

DP: It was Bill Foss, I think, who said that if Gary Sobers had turned up to play for us, he'd have batted 8 and been lucky to get a bowl until he'd proved himself.

'They didn't get on at all'

Favourite opposition characters...

DP: So many. Where do you want me to start? Taff, the Welshman (Blackboys), Albert Constable (Balcombe), Herbert Hunter (Penshurst), Aeneas Perkins (Underriver)...
JP: He stumped me legside off a quick bowler when he was 72.
DP: The bowler was 72?
JP: Aeneas.
DP: Such a nice man. Geoffrey Walford, too. He used to put us in his President's XI down there. At least six Invalids plus some proper cricketers... Bob Gale of Middlesex...

The Fernhurst Fireman recalled by Timbers and Kemp...

JT: ... went on duty at six, by which time he'd either bowled us out or scored 80. He was devastating, the scourge of any visiting side. It was mooted more than once, when we were about 5 down for 20, that we should set fire to the bloody pavilion!
JK: My recollection is he worked shifts. Sometimes he'd open the innings, get 40 then tuck his bat under his arm and march off and we'd think, where's he going? Then 'Oh yes, (fire drill) thank God!' He was considerably more proficient than his colleagues.

The Invalid Hundred.

DP: We had a problem with Brook House. They didn't rate us very highly. One occasion, I knew we were going to be up against it, so I got hold of Robert Burden, who'd played for Hampshire. I opened the batting with him and he was out before he got 10. I stayed there and didn't hit a four until I'd gone over 50 and then got an Invalid hundred. To my chagrin, I had this mate, Larry P. Yates, playing because we were one short. He always puts his foot in it – he shouted at me 'Take it steady, you've got to 95.' Well, of course I immediately stood away and was bowled.

JP: Who invented the Invalid hundred?

DP: It was some years ago, I forget where, Alastair got 70 and Eric Warburg got 100 and stayed there; didn't give anybody else a chance. We were all fed up and Alastair decreed an Invalid 100 was 94 or anything in between, i.e one shot away. Then you got out. I don't think Eric quite understood, he was a nice chap but … yes, Alastair brought in that rule and I've always stuck to it, but of course so many of you were rebels under my roof; you said, stuff Pritchett!

JP: Well there were moments when a real 100 was needed to get us out of gaol!

DP: But if you think about it, half-day cricket, if you get to 95, as I did at Brook House, that was enough and it was.

An Invalid recalls he was granted dispensation from this stringent club rule…

At Turville on his 40th birthday, he found himself 97 not out at tea. Totally knackered by the effort, he was presented with Phylosan which fortifies … etc. And was allowed by the soft-hearted opposition to have one over after tea to reach the coveted prize. He made no contact with the first four balls but on the fifth got the faintest edge. He knew it, Richard Butler umpiring knew it. Andrew Ingram, the Turville keeper, knew it but kept his mouth shut. Square leg made a half-hearted appeal. Butler's hand stayed resolutely in his pocket. The Invalid walked. 'Bad luck, old boy,' said John Shepherd, the scorer. All his team-mates applauded him for his sportsmanship, and the club rule remained unviolated.

Late one wet winter night, the phone rings in the Invalid's house. 'Shepherd here. Just glancing at the Turville match ... I added your score up wrong: 3 short.'

Lies, damned lies and statistics!

Another tale from Shepherd touching on the Invalid hundred ...

A game at Tatsfield, years ago. New fixture, John Timbers was running it. The pavilion looked like the last ten minutes of the fight in 'North of Alaska' [*sic*]. They couldn't find bails to put on the wicket, they couldn't find a ball, an umpire, they hadn't got any coats ... an absolute ruddy shambles. Pritch was playing, he was not best amused. Eventually the day got under way and David got an Invalid hundred, he got 95 and threw his wicket away. The Invalids won easily, we're in the pub afterwards ... and a nervous John Timbers approaches David, knowing the great man wasn't all that happy. 'David, they're asking for a fixture next year.' Pritch says, 'Tell them we're busy.'

This story, among many, was related on a winter evening in the warm and welcoming confines of the Churchill Arms in Notting Hill Gate – where Kevin Moore joins our story. By profession a Private Investigator, he doubled on occasions as an Invalid umpire. Kevin expounds:

My first encounter was Old v. Very Old Invalids ... at Underriver? I arrived, not knowing anybody, was introduced to Pritch and we got on famously. 'Nice to see you, we always need new people. How did you come

103

here?' 'I'm a friend of Bill Rodwell,' I said, 'and John Shepherd.' 'Really,' he said, and the conversation ceased.

Pritch takes a different line on this....

DP: John ... Kevin? Yes, well you could come from any direction and be an Invalid if you understood what *we* are about, as of course they did, as you will doubtless point out.

Pritch memories continued – Brook...

DP: We were one short, I was staying with this old friend of mine, George Cameron Douglas, who looked very much like a peppery Indian Army colonel. Alastair got him to play, and typical Alastair, he put him on the square leg boundary down the hill and George hadn't got any boots, he was in his leather soled shoes and of course Invalid bowling ... the thing got hit down to him regularly. George tried his best but kept falling over because of his shoes, and there was Langrishe, Belfrage and Pritchett in the slips roaring with laughter. George would pick up the ball in fury and say 'You buggers...' and after this happened a dozen times, he throws it in and it hits their umpire at square leg smack in the base of his skull. He clucked like a chicken, went down and we just went on laughing. It was appalling: the poor chap had to be carried off. That was the end of that fixture, because of our bad behaviour. We weren't required any more.
JP: Was that decided on the spot, or did it come in a Christmas card?
DP: I can't remember ... but, anyway, we were dismissed and quite rightly too.

Some noteworthy characters: Martin Meeson...

Nice man, I remember him getting out in the first over at Penshurst having made 26. But he suffered from the Unilever gang. There was a nasty chap (I won't name) took a fancy to Meeson's wife, very pretty. She went off with him for a time, and Martin never got over it. The last I heard he was running a bar in Ibiza, the wrong end of Ibiza.

David Rees...

A good friend, a very talented all-round sportsman, racquets, rugby, he was four years in the Clifton school side: he played against Tonbridge and Cowdrey at Lord's. He was too much of a gentleman to decimate the villages, but he never dropped a catch. He made a successful career as a Tea Merchant in Nairobi.

Ray Harrison...

I liked Ray. His wife I'd known out in Calcutta. Deanne, very attractive. Her father was the manager of the Great Eastern Hotel there, and she was one of the few girls about, in great demand. Ray married her back in England. Yes, I liked Ray and the division I spoke about earlier, that blew over eventually.

John Lund...

Yes, dear John. He opened the batting and he was a pretty good opening bowler. He came to the Invalids through

James Lipscombe (quite a hairy character) whom I'd met in the Stragglers. They'd played Yorkshire League together. But John chose our kind of cricket, I'm glad to say, and knew how to play absolutely to the right level. The villagers didn't see him as a ringer. They always appreciated a really classical batsman.

John Lund died at the age of 47. He had previously suffered a heart attack but seemed to be on the mend.

DP: He'd had flu and he died after lunch one day, in his armchair. There was a wonderful turnout at his funeral. Every club he'd played for on parade. He was a great mate of mine, but you see he was a good drinker. Perhaps he didn't look after himself.

JP: I remember him coming to Seagry in his last summer. He couldn't play on doctor's orders, but he umpired. I was batting, and he said quietly, 'One thing I want to do is go out and bat one more time and play a couple of the old shots.'

DP: When you think of the Invalids, you tend to think of the times when things went haywire, but you must also remember we did have some good cricket, and John Lund was invariably part of that.

The Invalids boast a number of players who fall into this category. Three spring immediately to mind and are included at this point, sparing their blushes.

Bob Bairamian...

At Dover College, where he was a galactic star in an underachieving cricket academy, Bob proved himself in countless arenas, as batsman and wily purveyor of the art of off-spin, from the shortest run in history (only Bomber Wells of Goucestershire could match it). Bob propelled the ball when the batsman was scarcely ready and chucked a few, so it was said, when the umpire wasn't looking. He paraded his roguish tricks with a flourish and a bonhomie which was hard to resist.

And he added a new dimension to the social side of our game. While Headmaster of Holmewood House preparatory school, near Tunbridge Wells, he engaged us in a fixture which usually stretched our resources beyond their capabilities. Why? Because among his staff could be found 'schoolmasters' with the cricketing pedigree of Bob Woolmer, Charles Rowe (of Kent and Glamorgan), Robert Burden and the terrifying Ed Flitton, the quickest bowler most of us had ever faced.

What Bob was saying was: don't settle for rustic incompetence, however charming that seems. Try harder! A schoolmasterly tone and a sharpish lesson for an Invalid. The club's credo from birth was never to get above itself or take its performance remotely seriously. But we know the satisfaction in playing well and even, dare we say it, winning a hard-fought contest or two. The ritual stuffing we got from Holmewood House was a prelude to one of the most enjoyable evenings on the Invalid calendar: the outflowing of Bob's hospitality in the afterglow of a satisfying victory for Bob.

Doctor Daryl Cantor...

Arguably the most famous Australian to play for the Invalids since the legendary W.A. Oldfield. Prone to lose his way to fixtures he's played in many times previously, his familiarity with the Dartford tunnel (but going in which direction?) has passed into Invalid folklore. But his most important contribution to cricket centred round his relationship with Kerry

Packer. Cantor, skippering his school, the famous Geelong Grammar Down Under, ran out a hapless young Packer for 0, dropped him from the next match for underachieving and took over his wicket-keeping duties.

At this formative moment in his life, Packer lit a smouldering fuse against the cricketing establishment which fully ignited years later. So you can trace everything that has happened since, the murky emphasis on money, match-fixing et al, down to that single misjudged call by Cantor. He still bats, keeps wicket and bowls to the highest Invalid standards. What he is less successful in doing is keeping his muscles intact. Barely a match goes by without a seizure of some sort in thigh or calf. This is not of course as funny to Cantor as it is to his team mates.

As amiable and relaxed a companion as you could hope to meet, there is nonetheless a ruthless Aussie streak in his nature, best illustrated by an incident recalled by Pritch.

Invalids v. *The Stage* at Hurlingham: August Bank Holiday Monday. They batted, we bowled them out for 110 and opened with Daryl and Jeremy Deedes. They reached 70 without trouble, then it started raining. I was umpire, I said, 'Look, we'd better go off,' and Daryl retorted, 'We're going to finish this match.' After another over or two *The Stage* were looking particularly bedraggled, all their make-up was running, they were in quite a state. So really for the sake of the fixture, I said, 'Look, we've *got* to go off.' I literally had to get hold of these two by the ears, and they were both equally angry with me – wanted to hit me with their cricket bats they were so annoyed – but we *had* to go off, we were all soaked to the skin!

108

'Look, we've got to go off'

Leo Cooper:

DP: I first met him in the Stragglers. I remember a game on
the Nore Command ground in Chatham, he got in such a state
before batting he was shovelling Librium into his mouth – but
when he got going, by George, he could hit the ball. He was
part of that great Radley-Dexter side. His wife, Jilly Cooper,
would turn up to decorate the proceedings. There was an

Ockley occasion ... we were all in the pavilion having tea. The opposition were the other side of the table, and there was Jilly in this string vest without a bra on. The village had never seen anything like this – not sure we had either!

JP: Leo quite cheerful about it?

DP: Yes, quite cheerful. I don't know whether it helped us or not.

An umpiring tale (from Rodmell) recounted by Jeremy Kemp...

If it struck any part of your anatomy, from your boot to your head, up went the finger at once. This was the guy who inspired Leo Cooper to make a famous observation. The square was protected from the cows by metal spikes with a wire around, and at the end of the match when the umpire had done I think seven of us, including Leo, but also six of them, we saw these fellows going out, carrying metal stakes and somebody said, 'What the hell are they going to do?' Leo said, 'Barbecue the umpire!'

This was not the same Rodmell umpire who revealed himself on one of our vistits to be an American Professor of Literature. An esteemed Anglophile to the extent that he had fallen in love with cricket and taught himself the rules, he had taken a long lease on Virginia Woolf's cottage, which was then, as now, a shrine to her memory. The stream you cross to get from the pub to the ground is the one in which she drowned herself, but it seems such a sad trickle now that it is hard to imagine how she achieved it.

More Rodmell melodies... Pritch recalls:

We lost the fixture, I don't know why, but we revived it through a friend of mine, James Hilliard, who lived in the village in a delightful cottage with his mother. James was an expert on food and he cooked us a wonderful lunch which was extremely difficult to drag oneself away from. More than once, we all went up to the ground totally drunk... I remember Lund fielding at mid-off: he had this simple catch, and by the time the ball got to his hands, they were together in prayer and he got a severe rap on the knuckles.

Richard Butler remembers:

On one occasion I had my (not totally solid) lunch interrupted and was sent off with another reluctant Invalid, with the strict instructions to open the innings and 'STAY THERE' until the rest of us arrive.

Some villages never shook off the spirit of the Squirearchy, and Rodmell was prime among them. Did we say never? The cows remain side on to the midwicket boundary as a tempting target. One Invalid recalls an innings he played of 76 which included nine direct hits on the rumps of these disinterested creatures. Virginia Woolf's cottage remains ... and the stream, the Abergavenny Arms ... but the American Professor has departed and so has James Hilliard, who died sadly in his fifties. And the village team is no longer a soft touch, we need to be pretty smart these days.

Back at lunch with Pritch and JP, the paté, every scrap of it, consumed.

JP: In the 50s and 60s, would you say the team came from quite a narrow class structure?

DP: Good God, no! I'd have been extremely angry if anybody suggested that we were class conscious or also good at cricket, I mean ... we had actors: some were quite good cricketers, but the other end of the team you had a chap like Bill Shine who could just not put one foot in front of the other, poor chap, the ball comes straight to him and he just couldn't get his feet together, but as long as a chap was pleasant, good fun...

JP: And got himself there.

DP: Well, that goes without saying.

JP: It's trying to get this broader view of why we do it – it can't just be about travelling miles to hit a cricket ball around a village green, can it?

DP: I don't think you want to start getting too politically correct or anything.

JP: No, but I want to dig deeper. Not just rely on the jokes.

DP: But doesn't comedy often show the deeper things, if properly handled? You mix it all together and see what comes out.

JP: OK. But what *does* come out? Can you sum up the Invalids?

DP: No, I don't think you can. That's the beauty of it. You can touch on things, the bits you remember, that stick in the mind. But drawing conclusions, why do you want to?

JP: Because I'm writing this book!

DP: I'm sure you'll bring some order to it. That's your skill.

JP: This is beginning to sound like running a game! What did you think of the BBC TV film of *England Their England*?

DP: Yes ... John Timbers got them to come and see me. I told them what to do, and of course they ignored it. Most of the programme was taken up with this tea interval where they lampooned the old general. They missed all the fun and drama of the blacksmith bowling and all three running for the catch in the same direction. It was very poor, and I would have thought certainly Jeremy Kemp would have made a lot better

Squire than that chap they got. Yes, I told them about it all and they didn't take a blind bit of notice.

JP: We've moved on from eccentric, period characters. Do we miss them? Have we lost our identity? Are we just like any other club these days?

DP: Well, all clubs have their eccentrics – we're nothing special. We've all had to move on. It's just a matter of how you do it. Some clubs ... The Stragglers Of Asia, for instance. Two years east of Suez was the qualification, well that's gone by the board. I'm not quite sure they should still be here, strictly speaking.

JP: But they've kept their heritage intact, I think. Their recent tour in India, tracing their roots, really cemented things.

DP: Oh well, that's good. Shiv Datt organised that, didn't he?

JP: Wonderfully, with his friends and contacts. I take your point about identity, but the old members always have influence, they usher the new ones in, like adopted sons. And by the same token, should the Invalids still exist? Not much of our literary heritage on view these days, and no wounded veterans. We're dodos, strictly speaking.

DP: Well, all right, you've got me there. But I still stand by some of what I say.

JP: One thing which sets the Invalids apart and has always astonished me. Other clubs recruit socially, from school backgrounds or their professions: Stage, Law Society, Band of Brothers, Stragglers ... and clubs formed through regional connections. But the Invalids come from all over the shop and something quite mysterious binds us together. We make life-lasting friends. There are certain taboos, of course, like it may not be wise to discuss politics. We leave them at home, or if we find fellow travellers, that's fine. But mostly these things don't register. For instance, I've never been clear how Richard Butler votes or what he does for a living. I've probably been told but it hasn't clicked in ... yet I'd count him as one of my dearest friends.

113

DP: Rank Hovis McDougal.

JP: Yes, something to do with them ... but what? There's no need to explore it further, whereas a lot of club cricket, you feel, is people talking about the week's work and deals and opportunities or whatever.

DP: Well, I hope not.

JP: But it happens – just as it does on the golf course?

DP: Not with me. They say Real Tennis is a way of getting business contacts, but I've played quite a lot with John Ritblat, who must be one of the most successful property men in the country. We keep it quite separate. Will you have another glass...?

JP: No, thanks, really... I'm driving home.

DP: I can safely say that I've done no business, but I've made more friends through cricket than anything else.

JP: Me too, which makes it very hard to know when to stop. I don't know how to judge it at all. I don't think I'll travel miles to umpire. And if I come to watch, I could become one of those sad creatures who always has his kit in the boot even after he's 80.

DP: For some, it's over when their bodies pack up.

JP: Yes. Tom Graveney said it wasn't the eyesight or the batting which stopped him, it was when the legs couldn't get him through the fielding. He tells of the day he was digging in his front garden, just after he had been recalled unexpectedly to England duty in his late thirties. Two boys cycled by and one said: 'That's Tom Graveney's house.' 'Yeh, I know,' said the other, 'but who's that old bloke digging his garden?'

DP: I haven't heard that one.

JP: The other thing that finishes some is pride in performance. There's the story of Ted Dexter playing a charity game shortly after retiring, hurling his bat against a dressing room wall in disgust, having made a perfectly acceptable 40 and saying, 'That's it!'

DP: But of course he had his golf.

JP: Maybe there's more dignity in golf, Nicklaus, Arnold

Palmer ... and tennis, the veterans' circuit when you can clown around and be treated with reverence and affection. But cricket doesn't offer you that, does it? You just miss the bloody ball and bowl rubbish and misfield. You can only be forgiven up to a point, before you find yourself not being asked anymore, and if you've been someone, that's miserable.

DP: So your kit remains in the boot?

JP: No, I'm still playing! I was interested when you signed off, David. Rather abruptly. You just stopped, and for a while you didn't come along to watch.

DP: Well, that was partly because I felt I wasn't thanked when I left. I was rather upset about that. I may have been hard and tough, but quite frankly you had to be, to keep things going.

JP: You felt people took you for granted?

DP: I wasn't just rude and unpleasant to all and sundry. I was also rude to Lund, to Langrishe, good friends, if I thought they were letting me down. Because, if you turn up fairly often with only eight or five people, then you may as well write the whole day off. But things are in quite good shape now, I gather.

JP: Yes. Our trip to the Dordogne was wonderful, absolutely amazing, two years running, we won all six matches.

DP: Well, against the French you bloody well should! But you're not taking victory too seriously, I hope.

JP: No. At the Oxford Cricket Festival, we lost all four.

DP: As long as we didn't disgrace ourselves. And you're all right for young recruits?

JP: Coming through fine. And the reliability is good at the moment, particularly with mobiles and easy communication.

Invalids v. Seagry (Wilts) 23 July 2000 ...

A delightful fixture, but a distance to travel and it's holiday time. After a fearful hammering last year, the match manager's attempt to strengthen his team hits rocky ground. The batting

115

looks sound but the bowling is wafer thin, even by Invalids' standards. For a grim moment it seems the match manager himself will shoulder the burden of first change with his overly friendly leg-spin which has recently been afflicted with the 'yips'. His search becomes ruthless. Good batsmen, loyal old friends, are rejected as bowlers are sought far and wide, to no avail. Two places to fill, four days to go, and the phone is ringing. The match manager's oldest pal, Carey Harrison, now Professor of Humor at Brooklyn College (he occupies the late Allen Ginsberg's office) is making a flying visit to England and he has played for the Invalids before (Harrison, that is, not Ginsberg). Would he play? Yes, by God! Could he bowl? Well, he'd been pitching in a veteran's baseball team with modest success, and he could bat if served a diet of full tosses. Yes! But he had no trousers, his girth had expanded and he was sporting a beard to match W.G. Grace's twin brother. The match manager clutches at straws. His pal's physical presence might at least give Seagry a fright.

So, just a bowler to find. John Timbers (after the Chelsea Arts Club lunch) agrees to play but points out that he's semi-retired. 'It's best if I don't do any stretching exercise,' he says, 'before the day, in case something gives out.' All settled. On the Thursday, the phone rings. It's George, a bowler of undisputed class who has heard, via the many distress calls percolating, that the Invalids are short and he'll play. Too late! The match manager regrets; then smiles. The Professor of Humor from Brooklyn College ... didn't a certain Mr Shakespeare Pollock once do the business long ago? Could 'history' repeat itself? All that is left is to find the Professor a pair of trousers.

The match report – Invalids v. Seagry, 23 July 2000.

Can pigs fly? Trousers were procured for the Professor of

116

Humor. Invalids, batting first, posted a brisk 217 for 5 by tea. This included two fiercely struck fours in an over by the Professor, batting 6 in a panama hat, before a ball landed on his toe in front of all three. Seagry started well in the chase. One piece of fielding saw the Professor lunge headlong to his left to stop a scorching hit in the gully, with the panama remaining firmly on his head.

Seagry fell behind but wickets weren't falling, and with 12 overs to go a tame draw beckoned. With a shrewd and final throw of the dice, the match manager turned to his spinners, Mr Timbers and the Professor.

Seagry went for it hammer and tong and a thrilling half hour ensued. With 10 balls to go, Timbers shivered the timbers and leapt high in the air with a banshee cry. The game was over. Timbers (2-60) and the Professor (3-30) had done the business, with five wickets between them, four of the victims lured down the track like the baker of Fordenden long ago and comprehensively stumped.

Several points emerged in the afterglow. John Timbers was seen scanning the fixture card for his next game. And the Professor confessed he hadn't bowled a ball for six years and even before that, never seriously. How could he have hit such a length? He was last seen strolling away in the night air, bidding fond farewells with a nonchalant raising of his panama ... to resume his European tour.

All in the pub reflected it was a game that had just about everything. Different levels of skills had flourished, and a certain level of eccentricity had found its place. The game was competitive but played with grace and good humour. It takes two sides to tango in this fashion. The village could have shut up shop but didn't, all thanks to Louie, Trevor, Richard, John and the men from Seagry for making the day such a pleasure.

As a final titbit the village learnt late in the evening that the Professor of Humor was none other than the son of the late Sir Rex Harrison and the much-admired actress, Lilli Palmer.

117

'The Professor of Humor'

Resuming Pritch and JP...

DP: It's good to see a lot of sons following their fathers.

JP: They're coming in well. Loads of them.

DP: Keeping the old spirit?

JP: Very much so, even when most of them can't really know what the old spirit was.

DP: The villages must take credit ... but can they survive in the way we remember? You're closer to this than I am, but isn't there a gulf developing between our older friends and the young lads who don't really know what we're about?

JP: There are signs of it in some places. But maybe it was always like that. The young ones grow to understand us with age!

DP: Yes, we need to keep helping them ... contributions, that sort of thing. Richard Butler sees to that, I'm glad to say. You can't turn up and expect to play on decent grounds and have the ladies lay on the teas and take it all for granted. It used to get me very angry when I saw that happening.

JP: I don't think it happens now.

DP: Good. Well, as long as you don't need a sergeant major to bully you ... I'm too old to do it now.

David Pritchett packed away his boots in 1987; but not into the boot of his car; which was taken up with his golf clubs.

Pritch

5

EWEN

The 'gift' of captaincy was passed to the 34-year-old Ewen Gilmour. It must have been quite a burden, since he and his beautiful wife Nicky were raising three (later four) young children at the time and he was climbing the slippery pole of merchant banking, but he carried it lightly; and what must have spared him some of the hassle was Pritch's stern insistence that the club be properly structured and, by some loose definition, democratically run. In his hand-over letter to all Invalids dated 7 March 1987, Pritch had set out a blueprint for the future. The days of lurching haphazardly from game to game, once part of the Invalid charm, were no longer practical. Other teams who didn't adapt to modern realities were seen to fall by the wayside. Even so, the organisation had to be benign and flexible, and this would be down to the personalities involved.

The committee evolved naturally. **Richard Butler** added Fixture Secretary to his role of Treasurer. David became President after the death of Ian Leslie, and **Clive Seigal** was appointed Dinner Secretary, though the job description here is inadequate. What happens off the field is a subtle business, but Seigal understands it perfectly. The club defines its character as much in the winter confines of **Halliwell's** bistro barge and **Nigel Windridge's** wine bars, as it does on the playing field. But wine bars, you may ask. Is Sir John turning in his grave? He shouldn't worry. London pubs have changed since his day, and the ladies (we hope) feel more at their ease.

A score of match managers were appointed to deal with the often brain-curdling task of picking teams: the numerous phone calls, often into answer machines which guarantee no answer. Some managers now scatter-gun e-mails, and those who respond promptly get picked. This saves on the phone bill but can lead to six left-handed batsmen, three of them wicket-keepers, no opening bowler and no-one you can ask to bat 8-11. Or vice versa. Team sheets are now diligently posted, so players can arrange lifts, and some managers even send in reports, just as the 'serious' clubs do.

Paul Southon was the first to set this uneasy precedent. Southon, by way of a reminder, is the most perfect definition of the Invalid team man. In fair weather or foul, on tour or in any confined dressing room, his sheer ebullience would raise the *Titanic*. This stems from his Naval background. As the years roll by and a bit of weight rolls on, Southon, with his Edward the Seventh beard and girth, maintains a lithe athleticism behind the stumps, and he is no mean left-handed bat. Against the Gloucestershire Gentlemen in the Oxford Festival 2000 – when the middle-order Invalid batting plunged into Davy Jones's locker, this son of the sea strode out and set about him with a determined brio for which his skipper will always be grateful. The Invalids were soundly beaten, but honour was salvaged.

Here is the End of Term report Southon penned and despatched to Butler on 27 September 1991.

Dear Richard,

Herewith cheque for £30 in respect of Blackboys, as requested. Excellent game ... nice pub, nice people and another excellent win with my 12th man, young Jonathan

122

Hall hitting a fine 138 not out – although in his defence he did sky the ball on 99 in accordance with club rules. Regrettably the same fielder who never looked like dropping me earlier off the same skier, never looked like catching Hall! He also took 2 wickets and as his dad (Anthony) took 4 I had no problem in providing 'free' beer all night to allcomers at the pub ... a talent that continues to ensure the presence of umpire and scorer at all my games.

Final score:	Jonathan Hall	138
	Invalids	92
	Blackboys	130
Result:	Hall won by 8 runs.	

In all humility, the success (i.e Hall's late selection) has to be laid firmly at the door of one Daryl Cantor who found that he had to be in Nairobi that weekend.

Cannot wait for spring to appear over the window sill.

Winter Well – love to Liz et famille,

As ever, Paul.

In the summer of 2000, the Invalids had 23 match managers to cover 40 fixtures – a recipe, you'd think, for cliques, divisions, disaster. It hasn't happened. Without tempting fate, you can put it down to charismatic leadership and the brand of cricket on offer.

Back to Gilmour...

... or 'Biggles' as John Shepherd christened him. Shepherd is of an age when he may be one of the few who can recall the fictional post First World War flying ace, created by Captain W.E. Johns. This bygone hero, now a dubious figure in terms of political correctness, is probably totally unknown to most present-day Invalids. Shepherd says 'Biggles' came from an early sighting of the youthful Gilmour standing, somewhere in Notting Hill, on the running board of an ancient Citroën, pipe clamped to mouth, scarf billowing from his neck, blond hair waving: dashing, debonair and leading from the front.

The Citroën has been replaced by an ancient red Mercedes, but the description holds. Scorebooks reveal that in the early 90s the powerhouse of the regular Invalid batting was starting to rust up. Those who once counted on four or more fifties a season were lucky to scrape three between them. Too frequently a good day's cricket depended on an exhilarating Gilmour blast, and the rule of the Invalid hundred was waived on a number of desperate occasions. With no competitive jealousies in the club, Gilmour in full flow adds nothing but joy to a day in the country.

In the 21st century now, our Captain, who carries modesty to its ultimate point, has been heard to mutter with some relief that, when available, Hooper, Hall, Casstles, Hicks, Cox, Belfrage, Marno and others, not least the ageless Dennis Williams, are with him to share the burden.

A conversation with Gilmour and Jeremy Paul gives a personal insight into his own story and matters arising...

JP: So you had the bat put in your hand ... when?
EG: There are photographs aged two. Playing with my father in the garden. I think my cricket reached its zenith aged eight, when I was really rather useful.
JP: What happened at school ?
EG: At Rugby ... got into the XI aged 16, had a reasonable season but I did my A levels and left the next term, having done Cambridge entrance so didn't have the two seasons when I like to think I might have...

124

Ewen Gilmour
(Photograph by John Timbers)

JP: Blossomed?
EG: Yes. The season when I was 17 I played mainly for Limpsfield. It was always a regret that I didn't star on the schoolboy scene.
JP: At school were you bowling as well?
EG: Oh no, only house matches. One of the beauties of the Invalids was that one was allowed to bat at 3 and would get

the occasional bowl, whereas for Limpsfield, I'd bat about 7, after six Tonbridge Cricketer Cup players and wouldn't often get in. But it was fun at that age, to play that standard of cricket.

JP: What happened at Cambridge?

EG: Played a lot of college cricket and some Crusaders (the University seconds) ... but didn't really get my act together. Too busy partying. Not sure I made much for the Crusaders, made a lot for the college. Every year we'd have hopes of doing well in the Cuppers, we tended to have a Blue every year, but our Cuppers always ended in...

JP: Tears?

EG: In tears. Once we played Emmanuel and had five or six of their Blues back in the hutch before they reached 50 and failed to win.

JP: Can you remember your first Invalids game?

EG: One tends to muddle into the other. I think I remember scoring about 20 in six balls and being very frustrated to get out to a triple bouncer. It was rather the story of my Invalids cricket for the first five years. I thought I found the bowling so easy...

JP: You underachieved...

EG: Spectacularly!

JP: I remember dropping down rather arrogantly from Richmond cricket into the Invalids and failing to score a run for some time.

EG: It happened to a lot of people...

JP: It was the wicket, I always said ... these village tracks, you can't play!

EG: And the eccentric bowling looked innocuous but seemed to bounce in the wrong place. It takes a long time to develop an Invalid cricketer. I think now aged 48...

JP: You've finally hacked it!

EG: Finally. It's block everything that's straight and hit the ones very hard off the wicket, and it doesn't matter if it's in the air because the boundaries are so short.

126

This conversation is taking place on the Keble College ground on the first day of the Oxford Millennium Festival in August 2000, for the best and most famous Wandering Clubs, which include teams from Holland, South Africa and America. The aim is to play the type of cricket which is built on friendship, skill and pride, and is without cynicism. The event is the brainchild of Geoffrey Hartley (Chairman of The Stragglers of Asia and an Invalid, which is most probably the reason they're here). It has been organised by Ben and Tim Brocklehurst at *The Cricketer* magazine – in aid of the Lord's Taverners charities.

The patron of the event, the late Lord Cowdrey of Tonbridge, wrote these poignant words for the official programme:

If I was given the choice of one more game of cricket to play on earth, I would choose a one day Club Cricket match, played on a tree ringed ground...

The home team wives arriving with hampers of delicious lunch and tea for our day ... the game every bit as enthusiastic as any Test cricket ... dashing stroke play ... on a bumpy outfield ... where the ball defeats a despairing hand and somehow finds its way through people's legs to the boundary. Much hilarity ... though the captain and bowler hopes that we cling to the important catches. Everyone taking pride in their performance.

I found it such a relief to play in a game where success and failure did not mean the end of the world. I relished a game where my low score, a dropped catch and some slightly indifferent bowling did not matter a jot. All for teasing as the jugs of beer flowed ... in the rustic old pavilion. An hour later, we'd be in the local inn for another beer or two, before making for home. I loved this style of cricket more than anything else.

The Invalids are playing the Yorkshire Gentlemen and are

under no illusions that they could be in for a tough four days. One of their rising stars, Duncan Cox, has majestically square cut the first ball of the match straight into the wicket-keeper's gloves. As a red-faced Cox trudges back to the pavilion, Gilmour and Paul are joined by Bill Rodwell, whose memory has just been jogged.

BR: Were you there for the famous duck scored by the friend of Daryl Cantor who was a Sheffield Shield cricketer...?
JP: Was it at Fernhurst?
BR: It was. He was in for about eight overs, played absolutely immaculately and he got the most stylish duck ever seen!
JP: I was there.
EG: Was he a moderately recent Sheffield Shield cricketer?
BR: Oh yes, he wasn't that old.

Rodwell drops in another memory...

BR: This was on the way to Holyport – Shepherd driving my Mini because in those days he didn't have a car of his own so he liked driving other people's. The other two occupants were John Lund and Neil Brown, you remember? The feisty Yorkshireman? We were talking about this and that and Pritch's name came up, and Neil said, 'D'you know, I've never met this fellow Pritch.' Shepherd said, 'Don't worry, I'll arrange for you to have an audience.'
EG: Pritch actually took rather a shine to Neil Brown. He liked the cricketing Yorkshireman.
JP: I've been trying to capture the essence of Pritch – what does one say?
EG: As I understand it, Alastair ran the whole show, then Pritch got some organisation into it which it desperately needed. Certainly when I joined, we would lose or draw nine

out of ten and were always in danger of not giving the opposition a match...

BR: Struggled week in, week out...

JP: We'd turn up with seven or eight, of which only about four would be sober – and they'd tend to be the young ones who had to hold the day together because the others weren't going to produce much beyond a gin and tonic for the square leg umpire. I remember a period thinking I'm not enjoying this much.

BR: But it did mean you batted and bowled!

EG: You were talking about Pritch ... not only did he produce organisation, but he was hugely popular with the villages. He may have given off a wonderful character from the 20s or the 1890s, but they adored him. All the older ones still ask tenderly after him. He would drink with the opposition, taking them on at that, and although people might think he was snobby, he wasn't at all.

JP: Yes, when we tackled the Invalids and the snobbery question, he denied it fervently. I then did a random check through my own time and discovered I could scarcely remember a black man playing, or a homosexual...

EG: Not knowingly!

JP: ... or anyone from a council estate, as far as I could see.

EG: Coming back to Neil Brown, the bluff Yorkshireman, Pritch approved of him enormously. He rather liked the idea of having a professional and the money in the boots – not that any money, of course, went into the boots – but this goes back to very old-fashioned cricket traditions.

JP: I'm glad we're getting a more rounded view of Pritch, which I hope to God he won't mind...

EG: I'm sure he won't.

JP: But there was a time, wasn't there, when the Pritch philosophy of cricket clashed a bit with the newcomers and there were one or two awkward moments? Richard (Butler) and I both had spats with Pritch, and we can't quite remember why.

129

EG: I remember <u>your</u> spat came when you got us playing the Shambling Derelicts which wasn't on the fixture card, and you put it in the scorebook.

JP: Oh God, yes!

EG: Playing under the name of the Invalids without the President's permission. The most innocent thing in the world and it couldn't have mattered a damn, but Pritch thought it was some sort of affront to his authority.

BR: It was his team, and the rules of behaviour were defined by him.

EG: If he'd been asked, I'm sure he'd have been quite relaxed and agreed to it.

JP: It was careless and stupid of me. Usually I tried not to upset him.

BR: Yes, we were on edge sometimes in his company.

EG: That may have been because he wasn't always well in his last years of playing. But the villages remember him with huge respect and affection. Albert Constable at Balcombe, the Seagry people, and at Penshurst, Ken Watters, Herbert Hunter and John Lambert, who all remember legendary sessions in The Spotted Dog at Speldhurst...

Back on the booze...

EG: You get a camaraderie with alcohol. With the villages where you don't possibly have a great deal in common, the one thing that loosens and also bonds the two sides is a love of drinking. It's a way of introducing people, an ice-breaker. Rather like Oxford here at the moment. Everybody getting fairly boozed-up last night. After we came back from The Lamb and Flag, I think I talked to a number of different people in the Keble bar, some I'd known before and some I hadn't. It's so much of the reason for being here.

JP: But tracing it back to the post-war days, I've been grap-

130

pling with the theory that almost the only release from the tension of service and the shaken-up lives was to go out and have a big piss-up, and the Invalids provided the perfect outlet.

BR: It happened before that with Squire, didn't it? For two decades!

EG: And I slightly argue on the shaken-up lives. Although a lot of them went through tough times, those who were in POW camps in Burma or wherever … the war was also quite exciting for young men in their twenties.

BR: And sometimes pretty boring. The vast majority of them spent three or four years after Dunkirk hanging around waiting for Normandy.

EG: Yes, a lot of boredom, then bursts of adrenalin. The big shock for them, I think, was the social change they found afterwards. That generation … they may not have come from very affluent homes, but young 'gentlemen', for want of a better word, didn't seem to worry about a great deal. Then they left the services, and it wasn't an easy world for them. They didn't really know what to do.

BR: A lot of them came back from working in the Far East … where drink was part of the social norm, it's what you did.

JP: Yes, Bill Foss raised this. He recalls that anyone who stayed in a pub after a game inevitably drove home fairly drunk. It hadn't caught on that it might not be a good idea.

EG: In fact, we'll be shot for saying this now … but if you were a practised drink-driver, I won't say that you were safe remotely, but actually you could do it – or at least you thought you could do it reasonably confidently. Again, in the 70s, when I was at university, there was a huge amount of drink-driving which the police seemed to entirely ignore. I don't remember any undergraduate killing anybody and not very many killing themselves, which is quite remarkable.

JP: It's the 60s Invalids I'm remembering: some of whom were seriously heavy drinkers … so, you're right, I can't apply the 'shattered by war' argument.

'Any time, any place, anywhere'

EG: No, they'd have been too young. They were deprived during the war ... but I put some of that 60s drinking again down to the lives they led, fairly leisured...

BR: ... didn't have to be on top form on Monday morning.

EG: Just thinking of the City in those days ... most people would leave fairly shortly after lunch on a Friday, and I don't think much work was done often on other afternoons. A huge change when you look at the City now. I can remember the Chairman of my bank banned port for lunch in the early 80s and was nick-named Scrooge.

BR: Was he able to enforce this?

EG: Yes, and almost nobody now drinks in the middle of the day unless it's some special retirement lunch, where everybody had put a pencil through the afternoon.

JP: So, to wrap up this question of 'booze', it's with us...

BR: ... any time, any place, anywhere.

JP: No deep theories need apply!

BR: Do we have any teetotallers among us?

JP: Richard Durden. He handles it beautifully.

It is now lunch at the Keble College ground. The players handle the bountiful flow of beer, each according to his judgement and capacity. Shortly after, Gilmour strikes a ball handsomely – a six on any village ground – and is comfortably caught at deep extra cover.

Paul Southon joins Paul and Rodwell as a dejected but philosophical Gilmour resumes his seat and brings out his pipe and tobacco.

PS: All this deep thinking ... bad for the concentration.

EG: No, I'd have played the same shot anyway. Lesson learnt.

JP: To change tack. Pritch told me the reason he walked

133

away from us so emphatically when he retired. He felt unappreciated.

EG: I never understood that.

PS: Didn't we give him a present?

EG: We gave him ... no, we didn't. I've got a suspicion he told me that he didn't want one, didn't want any pomp or ceremony, but would just shuffle off. But I should have insisted on it. We did give him the Jocelyn Galsworthy original a while later (the celebrated painting of the Invalids in action at Penshurst), which I'm sure he's thrilled about. But now I think he's much more relaxed...

BR: Mellowed.

EG: But again, talking about disputes within the club, Pritch always accepted there were two factions: the bohemian element, the actors and the writers, and his old guard friends, Lund and company. But they got on surprisingly well.

BR: Yes, there were definitely two camps.

EG: I think he liked that.

BR: People like Matthew Walters (BBC Radio Drama producer).

EG: Let's face it, he liked anyone who could play cricket!

BR: And Matthew was pretty high on that list! He could bowl fast or slow, he was a very good batsman and a more than useful wicket-keeper.

JP: The scorebooks tell the tale. Yes ... it's getting Pritch clear, that's what I'm after. He didn't bring in the new faces, did he? Others were providing the new energy.

BR: Not strictly true. He got Clive Seigal and John Leafe...

EG: Yes. Picked them up at Lord's. Pritch was having a net. He used to put half a crown on his stumps and challenge the young Middlesex professionals to knock it off. He was always gutsy, quite happy to take them on, and they were bloody sharp!

PS: Leafe and Seigal were in the next net. Pritch saw promise and snapped them up for the next game, I'm told!

EG: I remember Pritch and I going to a Stragglers cocktail party... I won't say with the specific idea of recruiting but certainly keeping a weather-eye open, and the direct result of that was Peter Salisbury! (Lt. Col. Peter Salisbury, an opening bat of fine pedigree who has brought class and durability to many an Invalid innings.)

JP: Pritch went rather off the Stragglers. Said he didn't want the Invalids going that route. I said, 'What do you mean, Pritch? We're not playing the same sort of cricket.'

EG: What he meant, I think, was he didn't want us tallying up wins or losses or averages or anything like that.

PS: Like serious clubs do!

EG: It should all be played for the glory of the moment.

BR: ... and faulty memories!

For the record, The Invalids scored 192 all out against the Yorkshire Gentlemen, with two fine knocks by Tony Hooper and Jonathan Hall to grace any stage – and five ducks. The Yorkshire Gentlemen cruised to a nine-wicket victory.

6

FAMILY MATTERS

Fathers and sons...

There can be no finer joy for a cricketing father than the
moment he walks down the pavilion steps for the first time
with his boy beside him. Those long summer evenings of graft
and toil and the occasional shattering of glass have finally paid
off. For a mother, too, there is a glow of pride – and a flutter
of mild concern when the boy threatens to outshine the man
in her life?

The Crondall game in May 2000 saw three sets of Invalids'
fathers and sons in action – an honourable tradition which had
begun with Sir John and his son Raglan (who may have simply
made up the numbers since his career didn't appear to kick
in). Currently on the list are two Halls, two Belfrages, a
Collins, a Morley Clarke, three Wilkinsons and three varieties
of Gilmour, with fledgling careers for a Windridge, a Marno,
a Jupe – not to mention a very young Hall and others pro-
liferating.

**Simon Collins remembers his own debut in the Old v. New
Invalid fixture, now mercifully defunct.**

I was 12 years old: the only time I ever played against
my father. In my school team as a leg spinner, I bowled

136

against the Invalids' best batsman at the time, the classy and formidable John Lund. The result was my first wicket. I still remember the post-match celebrations as Lund was teased for being got out by a 'babe'. And I can hear David Pritchett telling me that it didn't matter how many wickets I took in my career; the wicket of John Lund would always be the prize. I was not popular with my family when the vast quantities of what I was told was lemonade (shandy?) finally got to me and I spent most of that night over a sink. A true Invalids baptism!

Anthony Hall – and his sons Jonathan and Ben...

A fine and popular cricketer in his own right, Anthony introduced in the late 80s his two talented boys, Jonathan and Ben. Jonathan, as we have seen from Paul Southon's match report, is a wonderfully destructive batsman who bowls with serious intent; Ben, a wonderfully destructive quick bowler who bats with serious intent. Ben was once voted Young Cricketer of the Year. At Seagry he hit a ball over the pavilion, over the road beyond and, as one local observed, 'clean out of the bloody village'.*

Invalids v. Edenbridge – a few years back: Ben, opening the bowling against a more than useful village team, rips out the top four Edenbridge batsmen for 0. The fifth, their skipper, edges his first ball to Anthony Hall at slip, who drops it. The clock stands at ten to three ('....and is there honey still for tea?') The Invalid captain, horrified by the events and fearing no tea at all, whips Ben off with his analysis standing at 2-2-0-4. The captain then contrives, with some ingenuity, to

---

*This is not the furthest a cricket ball has been hit without touching the ground. The crown goes to a Wisbech batsman who struck the ball onto a lorry full of melons travelling up the A17, which fetched up in Newark, a distance of some 50 miles, before being unloaded – and dropped by a clumsy delivery boy.

manoeuvre the village score towards a hundred. Finally, he brings Ben back to finish it off, which he does with his second ball: the first being called 'no ball' by the petrified umpire. Ben's analysis reads 2.1-2-1-5. The Invalids are then bowled out for 90 and lose the match by 6 runs.

If this was a 'serious' club, the Captain would most likely have been hauled before a committee and, failing any coherent explanation, been relieved of the fixture. Instead, having snatched defeat from the jaws of victory, The Invalids were praised for making a jolly good game of it, and a fine night was had by all.

The Hall family live in a beautiful house in East Peckham. Each summer they've hosted a fantastic lunch, prior to the Underriver game. The sun always seems to shine and, like James Hilliard's lunch at Rodmell, the guests have no great inclination to go off and play cricket. While on holiday in America with his wife Karin in 1999, Anthony died suddenly from an undetected heart condition. To that moment, his fitness had seemed supreme. The shock was, and still is keenly felt by all who knew and loved him. In the summer, Karin hosted the lunch – in Anthony's memory.

The Belfrage boys...

Rupert and Crispian, first noted in these pages for stuffing grass up people's exhausts at White Waltham, are the sons of Julian Belfrage, whose style and cavalier approach to cricket personified the Invalids in the late 50s and 60s. Born into the theatre, Julian's matinee idol looks extended to a matinee idol cover drive which was a marvel to all when briefly sighted. His love of horses – he owned several – granted him membership of the Turf Club, where he arranged the Invalid 60th anniversary dinner, an event memorable for the number of the guests who finished up under the tables. His boys have inherited his looks, his panache and his love of cricket. Crispian has kept his gifts under wraps perhaps more than Rupert, who has emerged as an extremely fine batsman and opening bowler whose feats of stamina at times defy belief. These have been achieved by Rupert's dedication to running marathons all over the world for cancer research, in memory of his father, who lost his battle with it in 1992.

Rupert runs the game against Follies Farm Old Spots at Chiddingfold, and his engagingly eccentric leadership brings frequent wonder to the faces of his team mates. This year your guide received a phone call in early March. Rupert was choosing his team by mobile on a train journey through Devon. At the point where your guide was consulting his diary, the line went dead – and nothing more was heard of the matter. A few weeks before the game (9 July) someone said that Rupert had his team settled.

Your guide assumed he wasn't selected and, remembering it was his daughter's birthday, made other arrangements. The team sheet arrived in the post and his name was on it.

The Butler brothers...

Richard and Clive Butler, as any who know them will confirm, have been lynch-pins of the Invalid effort for the past 30 or more years. While various satellites and meteors whiz in and out, their relaxed and amused observance brings an air of stability to the proceedings. Richard is arguably the best and most consistent slow bowler the Invalids have ever produced. He is almost certainly the leading wicket taker in the club's history, though he would be the last person to claim it. His calm administration has been noted elsewhere. He makes sure the match managers don't slack in sending in their fees (currently a fiver a head for game and beer kitty), but more importantly he keeps relationships with the villages on an even

139

keel and is never slow to spot trouble and slip in a small donation.

Your guide and Clive Butler were the first Invalids to set foot on foreign soil when they walked out to open the batting in Javea in Spain in 1997, a tour organised by Anthony Hall. Clive claimed the first Invalid 50, his firm and purposeful driving well suited to the rough outfield, the short boundaries, the matting wicket and a friendly ex-pat attack which was enough to account for your guide, who registered the first duck on foreign soil.

The Christopherson brothers...

Radley-educated, Tom arrived as a young and decidedly quick bowler. He is also a class batsman. Peter is less flashy but a man you'd readily pick for all-round reliability.

They illustrate a classic modern dilemma. Both have successfully burgeoning careers and have decamped into the home counties with young families. Like their friends Tom Bayne, Robert Lanyon and Nick Caddick, who joined at roughly the same time, the reality persists that, however much they love the game and the company, there are other ways to spend a weekend. This produces an uncomfortable feeling for them as summer approaches each year. In Tom C's case, this discomfort often transmits to his back, frustrating him further. There seems no clear answer. They could play village/league cricket near their homes but it doesn't appeal. We are looking at a growing problem in the game. Even half a day's cricket is virtually a full day's commitment.

The villages are suffering too. Their young turks – those who remain – aren't keen to give up a whole weekend to cricket. They will play the Saturday league, but Sunday as well, when teams like the Invalids roll up? Why bother, especially if they feel excluded from some obscure and ancient joke which has no meaning for them? Their dads and uncles are often left with 13-year-olds to tackle these invaders from another world, who can sometimes be pretty formidable: which is not to say that they won't still spectacularly under-achieve. Witness, 1999 at Britwell Salome, when an Invalids team which on paper you'd back to give a strong Free Foresters a fair game, collapsed against a team you wouldn't bet on beating a bunch of Girl Guides.

Back to family matters. Ewen recalls his father, the fondly remembered Lt. Commander Pat Gilmour.

EG: He played for the Navy in 1946, when I think only two of the 22 at Lord's weren't either County or Test players. Other highlights were a trial for Scotland, but that was by mis-take after he'd hit 90 for his local team. As you know, he was a bowler: but he did a lot of batting in South Africa without taking it terribly seriously. The Navy found it too expensive to take the ships out, they used up too much fuel, so they filled their time playing cricket. The Old Man got his runs on hard South African wickets. He told me either he didn't wear a box or he didn't wear gloves, because he found them too hot.
JP: And after the Navy?
EG: A lot of ex-officers coming out, aged 40 ... it was hard, but he joined the National Mutual to sell life insurance. He didn't get paid a huge amount, but had a lovely life-style. Left his office in Sevenoaks, back home by six to play cricket with us in the garden. I'm rather envious. His generation probably had it right.
JP: I remember an almost blackened vintage bat he wielded – a family treasure now, I imagine. And his enthusiasm was a delight. Age didn't matter to him or his bat.
EG: In his final year, at the Rodmell game we turned out with five or six specialist Number 11 batsmen. The Old Man would

have been 69. I suppose he could still see reasonably. He batted Number 6, on merit. We lost four wickets very rapidly, the Old Man came in and we put on a hundred together with him scoring about ten. Tremendous effort. His last game was at Ide Hill, where he bowled 13 overs for about 30. He died of a heart attack in the garden a fortnight later. So he went out in fine style.

Malcolm Gilmour, Ewen's brother.

EG: I was three years older. If you wanted him to play cricket with you, you made damned sure you didn't bowl him out too early; and when he was bowling, you didn't hit the ball out of the garden. Yes, we got on extremely well, didn't quarrel, and quite often turned out together for the Invalids with the Old Man. I think we had the odd memorable partnership, but obviously not as many as we would have hoped, because he died, aged 27, tragically in South Africa.

Malcolm was on a mountain trek in South Africa, and the alarm was raised when he failed to return. For two days his fate was uncertain. On the third day, a Saturday, the Invalids were playing at Hurlingham.

David Pritchett describes the events:

We arrived at the ground to hear that Malcolm was missing. Ewen decided the only thing to do was to go out and play cricket. He was 60 not out at lunch. And that's when he got the news. Nicky came with it and told me. I went up to him and asked him what he wanted to do. He said 'I want to go and make a hundred for my brother.' He then batted so classically, so beautifully ... I was umpiring, I had tears in my eyes because it was quite extraordinary. He batted so well (*He made 146*), and the opposition didn't know the story, they didn't know what had hit them. It was beautiful batting, he had a sort of purpose ... it was absolutely wonderful, almost guided too. And then he came out and got changed, and he and Nicky drove back to Kent, to join the family.

7

'PANDORA'S BOX'

A late August day, wet, windy and grey
Stragglers arrive but no chance of play.
The game was called off just before lunch.
What shall we do we bedraggled bunch?
Pritch asked if John Lund and I'd play
For a team down in Sussex that very same day.
Into our cars we roared out of town
Straight for the rural and rain-free South Downs.
We fetched up inside a fine local inn
Where two other players were into the gin.
The two-thirty start found us still in the pub
Our Invalid team were looking for subs.
At tea we had mustered nine players in all
Including a youth who had not held a ball
And three of whom now we know to be strays
God moves as they say in mysterious ways.
We gave 'em a game, we might even have won
And I was invited (begged even, say some)
To join in the ranks of a club of repute
Whose record is proud, that none can dispute.
Companionship's all and in every game
We strengthen and nurture the bright friendship flame
All this for me began as by chance
But any true player has such a romance
To foster and treasure as long as he lives
Of the game that he loves and the joy that it gives.

144

In the hallowed tradition of Invalid poets before him (Squire, Blunden, Belloc, Chesterton et al.) **Mike Halliwell** describes his first game and the chapter heading is dedicated to **Pandora**, a friend of Rupert Belfrage who played for the Invalids when they were caught short against Holyport in the mid 1990s. All concern was focused on providing the gutsy lady with the proper equipment, not least a box, to the extent that nobody present can remember whether or not she scored.

Two more box stories from Nina Clarke (née Boyd)...

(1) Dad and Edward Bishop were practising in the nets in Royal Hospital Gardens in Chelsea and they only had one box between them, so when they swapped from bowling to batting they disappeared into the bushes together to pass it over. Mum and I, then a little girl, were on guard duty to make sure they weren't arrested for indecent exposure.

(2) Dad would hurl his cricket stuff down in the hall on returning from a match. There was a lot of it as he carried the team's spares and the boxes had a habit of spilling out of the bag. Mum got so fed up with tripping over them that one day she arranged a posy of violets in Dad's box and displayed it on the hall table.

Now follows a proper attempt to bring the women into focus...

Formerly known as the 'Ladies', a natural courtesy bestowed in the days when their male counterparts were referred to as gentlemen. The 'ladies' tag always carried a hint of condescension, even guilt. They have graced the game, smiling at male vanity and providing a symmetry and harmony (along

145

with the teas, for which the men are duly thankful) since leather first thudded into willow. But how do *they* view it?

Betty Boyd recalls...

The role of the Invalids women was to admire the feats of their men on the field. They found it much more interesting to chat, read the Sunday papers and snooze in the long grass. However they were dutiful, so they appointed a lookout who would prod the appropriate wife or girl-friend and say, 'Clap now, he has just got a wicket/hit a six/run someone out.

Scoring (Nina remembers)...

Mum was often the scorer in the 50s and so got all the gossip from her fellow scorer. She was scoring at Penshurst once with Lord de Lisle and Dudley's cowman. She had been warned to be extra complimentary about anyone with red hair, as they were probably related to the cowman. He himself was less than complimentary about the Lord, his employer.

Jack Squire and Nina...

I was a kid, puzzling one day over the numbers on the tallywag (the plates that went on the scoreboard). Jack Squire was good at talking to kids and we had a long conversation about the logic of things. I looked at the number 1 on a plate but on the back it was not the number 2. I asked Jack if this was reasonable. He later gave me a book of his poems, inscribed *Reasonably – Jack Squire*.

Unfortunately it was destroyed in a fire at my home many years later.

A veteran conjures up memories of the women in the 1970s (when the world was young)...

Halcyon days ... the opposition, distracted by a bevy of beauties from Julian Belfrage's famous theatrical agency, retrieving the ball from underneath a sunlounger containing a new rising star... The Invalids, accustomed to these delights, watching with detached amusement...

The veteran's wife points out crisply...

The 'wimin' were there on sufferance. Often left outside the pavilion waiting for a morsel, a crumb and a cold cuppa while the official tea was devoured by the players. Not invited (in those days) to the all male end of season 'knees up', treated with respect and courtesy, of course, but there only to adorn the day.

It is shameful to admit this lady had it about right, though times have hopefully changed. As 'women' these days, they are an altogether more resilient breed, and there seems to be fewer of them about, at least on the Invalid circuit.

Three types of women in cricket...

First, those who love and understand the game, as well as any man. The actress, Gillian Raine, the widow of the wonderful Leonard Rossiter, knows her cricket inside out. On a grey Monday afternoon in a BBC rehearsal room, she was once seen glancing anxiously at her watch. Would she be finished in time for the closing overs of Middlesex v Glamorgan? A game played in an eerily empty Lord's, the result of which would go almost unnoticed in the following morning's paper.

Then there are those who play. As our founder, Jack Squire, was sharp enough to note in the late 1930s, the girls were pretty hot stuff. His opinion was treated sceptically, but who would bet against the current England Woman's Test team beating a top club side nowadays?

Finally, there are those to whom fate has dealt a cruel hand. Falling in love with a bloody cricketer! What to do? Often it's their only day out together. A day ... out of their lives?

'The Wimin' circa 1955

Let us imagine...

'Jill' has just married 'Jack'. They adore each other. Jack adores his cricket. Jill drives out of town with Jack to some distant beauty spot where she will lose him for the day: he will be focused on his obsession. Jill has choices. If the sun is shining, she may simply lie back thinking of England or mingle pleasantly with others in her plight. If they are at Balcombe in late August, what fun to go picking blackberries together! She also has the car keys. She can drive away, missing Jack's triumphs/humiliations of which she will get an earful later. She has friends nearby, or a stately home to visit, or a monkey sanctuary? A day out. Fine. She will return to the pub where she will meet 'interesting' men who, if they notice her, will politely enquire after her well-being as she sips her orange juice, prior to driving her man home.

And if they have a baby, she can breast-feed on the boundary. Why not? An Invalid cricketer has a wife who, all their happy life together, has struggled to come to terms with cricket which she tolerates affectionately, as long as she's nowhere near it.

But one day she finds herself at Hurlingham with a toddler and a plastic potty on hand. A military gentleman is advancing on her in cavalry twills and a tweed jacket. Once a Colonel in the Indian Army, he is now on the Hurlingham Club committee. He demands the pot's instant removal. It is offending the membership. The wife gazes round. She sees no membership present. But rules are rules, madam.

On another occasion this same lady is persuaded to attend a charity game in which her husband is playing. It's a lavish affair with stalls and side shows, a tombola and the Red Devils due to parachute onto the wicket in the tea interval. There are 5000 spectators. The Invalid walks out to bat with Vivian Richards – unquestionably the highlight of his cricketing life. Where is his wife with the camera? Nowhere to be seen. She is buying

149

clothes from an Oxfam stand. The Invalid puts on a hundred with Viv, against international bowling: both reaching their fifties in the same over. On his dazed and triumphant return to the pavilion, the Invalid looks for wife and camera, in vain.

The following week, he modestly recounts his deeds to his friends in the White Rock pub at Underriver, but with no witnesses and no photographic evidence, his story is greeted sceptically, even sympathetically. As fantasies go, this one seems to have gone ballistic. Somewhat dashed, the Invalid goes out to bat and the village paceman has no difficulty bowling him, second ball.

Strange how this section, devoted to women, has slipped almost unnoticed back into the male perspective.

'Rules are rules, Madam'

As the writer Robyn Davidson observed: (*Against Travel Writing*)

A woman sets out into a world whose public domain is organised by and for men. How far can she claim a freedom of action taken for granted by her male counterpart, knowing that she is always, and everywhere, potentially prey? In the late 19th century, Isabelle Eberhardt solved the problem by dressing as a man when she travelled through the Sahara. Others waited to reach an age when their sex was no longer so desirable, when they could become, as it were, honorary men.

The last word? The nagging doubt persists that men should still make the day more appealing ... *but how?* By letting them umpire? Years back, Tom Tatham remembers being given out by a lady umpire – but what was she *doing* there? Girls have made up the numbers on occasions, as we've noted. But can we envisage a future when a mixed-sex team could be chosen on *merit*? Is this desirable?

'We'd have to play with smaller balls,' says Jack, downing his final pint of the night.

Sex scandals and matters arising...

Disappointingly few, or at least few that have risen to the surface. One incident did tickle the senses, however, for those who witnessed it.

An Invalid is batting rather well when, out of the corner of his eye, he sees his wife being led off into the bushes by a team mate who carries a certain reputation. The Invalid skipper spots this with dismay and for the sake of morale if nothing else, he details someone to follow them into the woods and BREAK IT UP! The player, deeply unhappy with this assignment which he feels should be the duty of the 12th Man (should there have been one), runs through a number of rapid permutations. The stern frontal approach: 'Come on, mate, there is a code'. The pragmatic/breezy: 'Sorry to butt in, but the skipper says you're in next'. The innocent/disarming: 'Is this a good spot for blackberries?'

Meanwhile, the batsman has an important decision to make. To get himself out and save his marriage, or continue his rich vein of form. Being the man that he is, he opts for the latter – and is dismissed on 96 (much to his fury) for an honourable Invalid hundred. The right decision? A few weeks later, the marriage is declared over, while the pleasure of the innings lingers on.

Sometimes sex rears its head before a match gets under way. Pritch recalls:

It was against the Grannies and we used to have some fair old tussles with Pougatch and Villiers-Smith ... they'd chuck in the odd Blue against us. The week before the match, I met a West Indian, quite a flamboyant chap, gold chains all over him, but he said he'd opened the batting for the West Indies and I was inclined to believe him. I thought this'll be splendid, he can come to play for us and we'll see what Pougatch makes of that. I was really looking forward to it, I would be happy to make him an Invalid. But of course the bloody chap didn't turn up. Apparently he was a well-known ladies man, so something obviously caught his eye and he couldn't be bothered with us.

Sex ... and pet tales:

The number of Invalids whose stroke was galvanised or put

152

off by the presence of the fair sex are legion. There are some whose performances have been witnessed by their dogs. John Leafe (Alsatian), Richard Knox Johnston (labrador), David and Belinda Pritchett (English pugs) and Jeremy Paul (golden retriever) spring to mind. Like the Tichbourne butler, the dogs can do the fielding and take on the job of watering the wicket. Someone once brought his parrot along. He'd taught it the art of umpiring and named it Dickie Bird. The ruse was that when his owner was bowling, 'Dickie' would be stationed on the top of the sightscreen and as the ball passed the bat, he would issue a loud 'snicking' sound, followed by him supporting his owner's vociferous appeal. 'HOWZAT!' With Pavlovian reflex, the startled umpire would raise his finger, the fielders would look bemused as the batsman trudged away, muttering darkly. This was successful on any number of occasions, until the day when Dickie, not fully concentrating, went through the familiar routine. Snick! 'Howzat!' The finger was raised … and the victim? His owner! Dickie Bird was last seen being driven away from the ground, screeching in a high falsetto.

On reflection, this could be a shaggy dog story.

8

'IT'LL ALL BE THE SAME':
'THE INVALID CENTENARY MATCH'

Don't forget Saturday morning Charing Cross Bullet* (runs the e-mail) 10.15 sharp whatever you do don't be late Gilmour.

For the record, the game is not taking place in 2020 (the exact year) but on a hot summer day in 2014 – an Invalid centenary, being six years or one shot away.

The venue of the match has been the subject of lively debate. Though the game of cricket has changed little, England has changed dramatically around it, geographically and ecologically. Gone are the days of the motor car spewing out fumes in clogged country roads. Gone, the dodgy weekend return from the quaint English village. Gone, indeed, is the quaint English village, swamped by redevelopment and water.

Where to play? Underriver is gone, under its river. At Rodmell-on-Sea, the tide seriously curtails the hours of play. Blackboys has been submerged into Uckfield. Nettlebed & Swyncombe have become Nettlebed & Swyncombe & Britwell Salome & Turville. They are now called NSBSTCC for short; having lost all their grounds, they play at Moreton-cum-Middleton Stoney.

---

*The Bullet has replaced the London Underground. Extremely clean and efficient, it gets you from Rotherhithe to Rayners Lane in 14 minutes.

Just one much loved venue survives. Its backdrop is the stately Penshurst Place, preserved at the tax-payers' expense by Euro-Heritage. No matter that our friendly old rivals have merged with Edenbridge and Cowden and call themselves Kentsmead CC, they'd be delighted to play host.

And back in fashion is the charabanc! The team gathers for a high-speed conveyance down super-charged highways, pollution-free. Shame that they can't stop for a quick one at Catford or the White Hart at Sevenoaks; but the cares of drinking and driving are banished for ever. They travel their own booze – barrels of real ale and whatever – a nostalgic tilt back to the heady days of the 50s and 60s when the booze was in the boot. The match is scheduled to start at 11.30. After a frenzy of mobile activity (you speak now through the signet ring on your left little finger) the team starts to muster. Even though Inner London is a centre of tranquillity, with happy citizens gliding about on solar-powered walkways, the Invalids are still two players short. The charabanc finally leaves Charing Cross at 12.30 (without Rupert Belfrage and James Gilmour) to travel the 50 miles into cricket history.

Out on the open road, the charabanc, humming along on methane, reaches the former village of Penshurst in 40 minutes flat. The ground, the charming pavilion (preserved by Euro-Heritage), the cloned cattle grazing in pasture and Penshurst Place itself daubed in hazy sunlight stretch out in welcome but this sublime picture, evoking such memories of Squire's England long ago, is shattered by the presence of several vehicles, disgorging hoards of excitable, elderly gentlemen.

From the window of the charabanc, Sir Ewen Gilmour, aged 61, and flushed with a recent golden retirement, recognises old friends. Some he could have sworn were dead, but here they are, larger than life, being propelled towards...

...An ancient wooden stile, flanked by strips of cattle-restricting power-fencing which only a fool would touch. This obstacle has to be surmounted, for any sort of view of the game. It's a teaser, and much jabbering has broken out as a team of carers and nurses ponder their options.

Gilmour glances at the Dinner Secretary, Duncan Cox whose idea it was to round up all surviving Invalids for this day of days. In spite of the technology at his fingertips, Cox has spent a nightmare six months putting this audacious plan together. It has involved a tedious trawl round the 'Twilight Homes for the Infirm and Bewildered' and a desolate scanning of the obituary columns of the *Daily Telegraph*. Some who RSVP'd back in January have regrettably RIP'd by June. Even so, 94 ex-Invalids are now clamouring to be winched over the innocent stile. (The number is touchingly ironic, a wag points out, being one shot away...)

'Hoards of excitable elderly gentlemen'

The players emerge from the charabanc, claiming their aluminium 'coffins' with their names emblazoned in blue and old gold. The last to appear is Mr Mervyn Jupe, primed to the armpits with the latest, state of the art, umpiring technology.*

It has been agreed to play 12-a-side when Deanne Largan, the current Number 3 in the England Women's Test team and the fiancée of a recent Invalid recruit, announced her availability, finding herself with a rare day off.

Kentsmead have graciously acceded to this and swiftly pulled in the current Australian fast bowler, Glenda McGrath, to balance the numbers. Glenda, on a three month course studying midwifery at Kent University, has recently had her quickest delivery timed at 149.2 kph (92.3 in old miles).

As the charabanc driver pulls out, promising a late pick-up, Gilmour tackles the problems confronting him. Not only can he not reach the pavilion, baulked by the log-jam at the stile, but over the heads of his ancient pals, he can see a game already in progress. Demonstrating a fitness beyond his years, he leaps over the power-fencing. Catching his foot and bravely absorbing the shock, he races across the outfield to confront the Kentsmead skipper.

'What are *these* people doing here?'

'What are *you* doing here?' is the phlegmatic reply.

'Playing *you!*'

'Not *today. Next* Sunday.'

'*Oh ... God!*'

Gilmour gazes at the Fixture Secretary, Clive Seigal who is hobbling up behind him. Seigal's elevation from Dinner to Fixture secretary in 2006 may seem a somewhat 'pyrrhic' promotion – but after the emphatic retirement of Richard Butler there simply were no other candidates.

---

*It should be stated – in the light of what is shortly to follow – that all human error has been eradicated from the cricket umpire. All decisions are now made scientifically so none can be questioned. This has revived the old-fashioned tradition of sportsmanship and has generally been accepted as a benefit to the game.

At the party celebrating Butler's retirement, held on 10 October 2006, in an ante-room at the Royal Opera House where Gilmour is on the Board of Governors, the old boy was presented with six Jocelyn Galsworthy originals (which he most generously put up for auction in aid of a new Blackboys-cum-Uckfield pavilion) and a silver chalice inscribed RJM Butler 994, the number of wickets it is believed he had taken for the Invalids. After a medley of Sir Noel Coward and Sir Cliff Richard songs performed on the night by the veteran entertainers, Rodwell and Jupe, John Shepherd had been helped to his feet by his friend Kevin Moore, to announce that a trawl through the scorebooks (several pages missing) had revealed that the Butler wicket tally was wrong: it had fallen, at least, 6 short.

Back in the present, the hapless Seigal and Cox wilt under the steely gaze of their Captain, but before recriminations can be launched, another figure enters the arena. By hook or by crook (and with the latest resources of modern gadgetry), a laser-driven wheelchair is seen hurtling across the outfield, narrowly missing long-off. In it sits the much venerated President, almost out of his seat. In valiant pursuit are several white-coated figures, a mechanic, the President's wife and three English pugs.

'NOW LOOK HERE!'

Whether it is the stentorian bark of supreme authority or the menacing presence of the pugs, the result is swift and decisive. Bad light at once calls a halt to the play, and eleven confused cricketers are sent packing.

At the stile they pass nine fresh cricketers and a young woman. Following on, are a swarm of geriatrics in various states of mobility; and behind them now sprint Rupert Belfrage and James Gilmour, who met by chance at the Charing Cross Bullet station and 'flew' down to their appointment with destiny, landing on the site of the Leicester Arms, Penshurst, once favoured by Invalids, now awaiting development into a 'state of the age' sewage farm.

158

As they reach the steps of the charming pavilion, the Invalids, hearing of the fixture confusion, heave a hugh collective sigh of relief. Glenda McGrath, the subject of much terrified debate on the journey down, won't make it. Will she? They see the Kentsmead skipper making frantic calls through the signet ring of his little left finger... But all they have to do now is win the toss and bat.

They lose the toss. Kentsmead will bat. Gilmour returns to confirm the grim news. Pipe firmly in mouth, stoic and resolute, like some First World War flying ace in an old British movie, he hides his darkest fears from his men who anxiously consult their digital Rolexes. At a fair estimate, the feared Aussiette cannot arrive before tea? But travel is so damned quick these days.

'We'll have to bowl 'em out fast,' Tony Hooper mutters. 'Get stuck in and get it over before she gets here,' is the general consensus.

In the last Test Match, England Women v. Australia in Perth, McGrath took 9-28. Only Deanne Largan stood firm with a gritty 17 not out. With this comforting knowledge, all Invalids turn their gaze towards Deanne, their high priestess, champion, belle of the ball. She smiles demurely. They usher her into the cramped stuffiness of the historic dressing room (preserved by Euro-Heritage) and stand waiting outside, as gentlemen do. After fifteen minutes she emerges, radiant and ready for action, as they scramble in past her.

Thirty minutes later, Gilmour steps blinking from the dark recess (*something* must be done about getting these people proper light, for God's sake, in this day and age)! Stuffing his pipe (with tobacco flown in from Rattray's in Perth), he turns to the President, the link with the glorious past, in a plea for guidance. *How do we play this?* The President solemnly waves him over.

'I couldn't care less if we win or lose as long as we put up a good show, because you know they're watching.'

Gilmour glances at the garrulous old gentlemen gathering round him, then sees the President's finger pointing upwards... Into the cloudless sky.

'Up *there*!'

Of course! Sir John Squire... Alastair Boyd... *All* the heroes of old! This one's for *them*! Game on!

At twenty minutes to 3, Mervyn Jupe strides out to the middle with his colleague for the day. They wear cardinal-red coats to distinguish them from the medics on the boundary and to stamp their authority on the day. As the Invalids shamble out, Gilmour is distracted by a stooping, bald-headed old fellow tapping his shoulder. To his alarm he recognises a former playmate.

'Ewen ... listen, in case of emergency, I do have my boots in the...'

'Thank you, Jeremy, but actually, I don't think...'

Gilmour hurries away and deploys his men. A voice yells out from the boundary. Gilmour turns and sees Bill Rodwell waving his stick. The Kentsmead opener...

'What about him?' shouts Gilmour.

'He's an Aussie! A Sheffield Shield cricketer!'

And the old quiz king is right! Strongly tipped for the Australian Test team just two years back, the man taking guard is currently employed as a gardener in Penshurst Place.

Ben Hall measures out his run. A hush. Four steps into his delivery stride, there is a piercing whistle, a light flashes and a robotic squawk rends the air. 'NO BALL!' Jupe jumps in alarm, Ben jams on the brakes. All eyes swivel towards the respected umpire as a thin spiral of steam rises up from his head. Rattled, Jupe makes the old-fashioned gesture of 'ball void': not a tough decision since the ball is still in the bowler's hand. Fortunately, the Invalid team contains several sophisticated technical wizards who rush to Jupe's aid and start to untangle – then reassemble the trembling adjudicator.

After a delay of eight minutes – at twelve minutes to 3 precisely – the first ball of the Invalid Centenary match is delivered. With the composure of one who has tasted the big time, the Sheffield Shield antipodean steps back to defend it. But, misreading a bounce not familiar to him on the wickets of his homeland, he is hit on the pads low down, plumb in front of all three of his stumps. Eleven men and one young woman leap high and punch the air.

They are greeted with a deathly silence. They stare at Jupe who is attempting to activate some controls manually. The silence persists. Jupe can only shrug helplessly. The phlegmatic Aussie steps out, prods the pitch and prepares to continue.

Early wickets tumble, some indisputably caught or bowled. Two, inexplicably, removed by the piercing whistle and the flashing light. One is the Sheffield Shield star, caught behind off his helmet for 8 – poetic justice, it is quietly acknowledged. At 3.40, Kentsmead are staring down the barrel at 69 for 7.

One hour and 20 minutes later, tea is taken with their total at 249 for 7. The reason for this turn-about is the arrival, at Number 9 for Kentsmead, of Saqlain Youhana, a Pakistan Test batsman who recently took an effortless hundred off the West Indies in Barbados and is currently employed at Penshurst Place as a librarian. His personal score stands at 148 not out. 'Our secret weapon,' smirks the Kentsmead skipper.

Only Deanne Largan with seven overs of beguiling leg-spin has slowed down the rampant destroyer. Her Captain has five times regretted putting his hands in the line of drives fizzing their way to the boundary. Others have been more prudent. It should also be noted that the guardians on the fence have earned their corn by leaping about protecting their charges. Just one got has through and this ended up in the right hand of Clive Butler – a perfect catch, warmly applauded.

One other point of interest – half an hour before the tea

interval, a strange sound began drifting over the ground. At first all eyes turned to Jupe, but he shook his head vehemently: he had 'switched himself off'. Was it the low murmur of cloned cattle coming up for organic milking? Not so. A head count conducted by Edward Marno from deep square leg, revealed that 78 of the 94 old Invalids present were soundly asleep.

In the time-honoured tradition, tea is 'sensational and prolonged'. As the Invalid players wipe the final crumbs from their mouths, they spy with a sudden collective chill a tall and rangy figure bounding towards them. Track-suited in green and yellow, her blonde pony-tail swinging fiercely behind her, Glenda McGrath has timed her arrival to perfection. Behind the super-heroine come her agent and her personal trainer, both loaded with baggage plastered with sponsor-logos (is there *nothing* this wholesome girl hasn't endorsed ?) and a flotilla of cameramen.

'Hi, Glenny'

'Hiya, Dee'

More a snarl than a greeting, Ms Largan and Ms McGrath peck cheeks and turn sharply on their heels. What's this all about?*

Gilmour hurriedly shepherds his troops into the dressing room where they huddle. After several minutes they emerge. It has been swiftly decided to resurrect an Invalid tradition, only once previously employed, years ago in a place called Charterhouse. They will decide the batting order by lot. Slips of paper numbered one to twelve are placed in an Invalid cap and shaken vigorously.

Gilmour looks around and by one of those odd quirks of fate sees 85-year old John Divett slipping the last piece of

---

*When poised to grab all ten wickets at Perth on 26 November, 2013 McGrath had Largan faintly edging the famed late away-dipper into the keeper's gloves – and refusing to walk. Twice! 'Where was the f**** technology? On the f**** blink?' This was the gist of the post-match interview beamed across several continents.

chocolate cake into his mouth. As the man solely responsible for this hallowed but contentious tradition, 'Speedy' is pressed into drawing the numbers.

At ten minutes to 6, Sir Ewen Gilmour prepares to face the first ball of the innings, chasing 250 to win in a little under two hours. Helmeted for the first time in his long and distinguished career, the Captain is also musing on his own mortality, not least his value to the team. Mentally scanning his last seven innings in this historic season, 4, 0, 4, 0 not out, 0, 4 not out, 18 (*oh yes, those three sixes!*), he takes reassurance from his opening partner, the quizzically smiling Andrew Casstles, now in his Invalid prime.

Jupe, who has spent most of the tea interval reprogramming himself, stands at the bowler's end in the fond belief this has been achieved satisfactorily. Glenda McGrath marks out her run which brings her perilously close to the President of the Invalids CC.

'What's that *girl* doing here?' says the President with incredulity.

'She's *playing*, dear' says the President's wife.

'Playing at *what*?'

'At *cricket*, dear.'

As McGrath scuffs on the grass, three English pugs growl at her suspiciously. She stares them into whimpering submission.

'PLAY!' roars Jupe.

Time does not permit a ball-by-ball account of what follows. A few selected highlights will serve: starting with the first three balls of the opening over which fly one bounce over the wicket-keeper's head to the boundary, each accompanied by the piercing whistle and the flashing light.

Reducing her pace slightly, McGrath's first legitimate ball is hooked over the square leg boundary by Gilmour, who later admits that he was taking avoiding action. At the end of the first over the Invalid score stands at 36 for 0, 24 of them extras.

163

At the end of Glenda McGrath's fourth over, her figures read 0-77. She has had 9 catches dropped in the slips, through which the majority of the runs have flowed. It is hard to know who has been more traumatised, the batsmen or the fielders. Usually competent at their level of the game, the Kentsmead slip cordon are counting their fingers and at least two of them are off seeking medical attention (which, given the age and needs of the spectators, is mercifully to hand).

McGrath storms angrily off to square leg, where she is surrounded by a clutch of drooling old men clamouring for her autograph. She tells them all to b***** off!

With 20 overs to go, the Invalids are sitting pretty. Gilmour has gone for 51, Casstles for 38, and there has been a familiar mid-order collapse, but the score is standing at a healthy (in Invalid terms) 127-7. Hooper and Jonathan Hall, both in their Invalid prime, are batting with easy assurance. With 12 balls left and only 14 needed, a series of slight blips occur. Hooper hits the ball firmly into his pads and is flashed out LBW. He walks off, a picture of controlled emotion. Those old enough to recall, conjure up the demeanour of a former England captain, Sir Nasser Hussain, CBE. Seconds later, a bat is sent crashing through the dressing room window, shards of glass showering some nearby elderly gentlemen. Nobody turns a hair (having scarcely a hair to turn between them). All rheumy eyes are fixed on the action. On the last ball of the penultimate over, Hall is run out strolling a run to mid-wicket, failing to notice McGrath swoop and hurl in a rocket throw which shatters all three stumps at the bowler's end from almost side on.

One over left, 10 to win. At the sight of Deanne Largan coming to the wicket, McGrath grabs the ball from her Captain's indecisive grasp and marks out her run. A grudge is on the point of being settled. The Invalid Number 10, Rupert Belfrage comes to offer the England Number 3 a word of avuncular advice. She smiles at him sweetly and takes her guard. The slips and wicket-keeper, sensing something's afoot (but what?), retreat another ten paces.

On the boundary's edge, the tension is mounting. Substantial bets are being placed and a number of chamber pots appear in view. The English pugs rouse their master from a brief siesta. They growl cautiously at McGrath. She growls back.

'That young woman...?'

'*Shush*, dear!' says the President's wife.

First ball ... a slower one? The England Number 3 drives it exquisitely through the covers for four. Her Captain gazes in wonder, then joins in the wild applause, hugging his beloved wife, tears in their eyes, as all the fond memories come flooding back to them... Days in a Kentish garden long ago... Joyful Sunday nets in their Wimbledon garden... Now, a moment for absent loved ones; who include a number of the Invalid family. Shameless emotions on this day of days. They wave to their old friend, Judge Wilkinson* (whose sons, James and Nick, have both been flashed out, having appeared to commit no offence, the injustice of it)!

Out in the middle, Ms McGrath eyeballs Ms Largan from a distance of no more than a metre. Words are flying. The close fielders clamp their hands to their ears. Belfrage, grinning, applauds his partner.

'Stay out of this, Pom!'

Second ball, straight for the throat, no prisoners. Largan dodges; her gum-shield spins from her mouth, missing her leg stump by a whisker. She coolly replaces the shield. Settles. Ball three, the famed away-dipper, cuts off the seam and veers sharply. The bat withdrawn – a late judgement? Three to go, 6 to win. The sun is dipping and a soft breeze quells the turbulent heat of the day. Was there ever a Test Match such as this?

---

*Lord Wilkinson is best known for his stern but humane judgement in the notorious case of Lord X who, in April 2008, was charged with a spanking offence which shocked a nation. The young woman in question... (But this is another story.)

Ball four... 'NO BALL!' Whistle, lights, as the ball spins out of the keeper's grasp. Two runs garnered. Ball four again. High and wide, safe to leave.

'Bottled it, Glen?' Sweetly delivered. A scowl returned. Ball five, the fastest ever (in this form of cricket), rapping the glove, Largan misjudging. The ball drops loose. 'RUN!' Yells Belfrage, and hears a soft low whisper.

'Over to you, Uncle.'

Four to win off the final ball. Was ever Rupert Belfrage born for this moment! As he watches the Aussiette striding back to the end of her formidable run, thoughts flash through his mind, the early days of uncertainty, when he stuffed grass up the exhausts, and... A girl called Pandora? His father, Julian in the world of theatre, so much the spirit of this team... Running marathons in his memory... 'This one's for you, Dad!'

'THWACK!'

Like a rocket from a space launch to Mars, the ball blasts off the Belfrage bat up .... up into the stratosphere to meet the angels, the unseen spectators, the ghosts of Invalids past... The hushed spectators crane their necks, spellbound as... Oh no, oh Lord, let the wind take it! Befrage and Gilmour scamper the first run... Oh, this matters!

Why? Who gives a damn?

Well, a global television audience, that's who! The game has come far from those humble Hambledon beginnings, and Glenda McGrath is a girl of her times. She's struck a deal, world-wide. The hidden cameras are everywhere, in the rafters of the charming pavilion, in the devices strapped to Jupe (without his knowledge in the tea interval): inside discreetly placed chamber pots, and the piece of chocolate cake which Divett inadvertently swallowed...

Meanwhile, the President of The Invalids Cricket Club is giving an impromptu interview to a reporter from CNN News.

'OK, now, Mr President ... your game of cricket. We

166

Americans, we love it, but we really wanna learn the grass roots...?'

'*What?*'

'The grass roots, Mr President ... excuse me, could you just keep those dogs under control? Thank you... How it all began for you. Why Invalid...?'

'Shush!'

'Oh ... Mrs President? Maybe, could you explain...?'

'Watch the ball!'

'The ball? Sure, the ball... Heck, we know about the *ball*...'

It's up there, swirling about; all resting on the outcome of its downward projection. And the world is caring too: since tea they've been watching every ball from Katmandu to Timbuktoo, from Tokyo to Kentucky ... there are heroes and villains out there!

'Get the Aussie bitch!' (This, an e-mail from Iowa, countered by...)

'Get those Limeys!' (From South Carolina: still smarting from the English betrayal in the American Civil War.)

!@!*!*#*%! (From Japan – but no translation to hand.)

'OK now, Mr President, we have world interest here...'

'What are you talking about?'

Three Kentsmead cricketers have positioned themselves under the ball. Largan and Belfrage turn for the second run and suddenly a voice cries out:

'Leave it to Thompson!'

Now it will be recalled that Neville Cardus told of the time when Sir John Squire shouted the very same name for a catch. But Thompson wasn't playing. And he isn't playing today, eighty years on. Was it a voice from the sky? Later, in the dying embers of the day, the Kentsmead skipper will swear that he never uttered the name. He didn't know any Thompson!

The three players under the ball hesitate, disperse, then

seized with doubt reassemble. They are joined by a fourth, the redoubtable McGrath screaming, 'MINE!'

There are some commands in life you don't mess with. But McGrath, circling the fast dropping ball with ferocious determination, is suddenly sent flying by the arrival of a fifth player. 'No, it is _mine_!' cries out Saqlain Youhana who, diving between the legs of the sprawling superstar, clutches the ball inches away from her groin.

At the precise moment Largan and Belfrage, plunging for the winning run, collide and fall in a heap. The match is over. A stunned silence, then the celebrations begin.

'Did we win?' murmers the President.

'We lost, ' says the President's wife.

The President smiles and turns to the American newsman.

'You can tell your people. *That's* what it's all about.'

CLOSURE

'GOOD GOD, SAID GOD...'

Visiting aliens and most Americans, confronted with cricket (with the exception of Sir John Paul Getty) can only turn away with a shake of the head. The veteran Hollywood film director, Irvin Kershner (*The Empire Strikes Back* among his credits), exclaimed loudly, when encountering the game for the first time on British TV last summer, (Atherton was playing his valedictory innings)...

'People do this for a *living*? And people pay to *watch*?'

Not to watch us, but what can we say to the unbelievers? So much energy and money spent on what can at best be described as a marginal pursuit in the greater game of life, weekend upon summer weekend, enduring the frustrations of weather and travel and as often as not, God help us, poor performance... Sagging bodies grimly defying the march of time and all human logic?

'What do you get back? What's the Closure?' Says Kershner, a maverick Europhile with a Ukrainian family background. 'Closure', it should be explained, is the Hollywood term for the feel-good factor an audience must have at the end of a movie, to ensure its success at the box office. Without it, you're dead.

What makes us feel good? The forging of unlikely and enduring friendships; the breaking of shackles, the broadening of views; the feeling of health and well-being; the shared awakening of something lost in youth, and that small nugget of achievement which, if we get it, transports us through a week or even a bleak mid-winter; the sense of self-worth and self-mockery (as we all become 'Characters' in some form or other); and the rich source of humour bandied about, given and received without offence.

Cricket is God in another form, a wise man once said. (Confucius?) It's the Omniscient Presence, mildly tolerant or blithely indifferent to mortals messing about with it, passing the time before eternity.

John Paul Getty at his home at Wormsley has taken this notion a step further by creating a cricket paradise on earth (by invitation only) where the sun always shines and the champagne flows over a lunch to die for, and you can rub shoulders with old masters of the game, his guests, reminiscing at their ease, their heroic deeds recorded for ever.

But back to earth for a final thought. Sir Derek Birley's estimable book *A Social History of English Cricket* consigns village cricket to an Epilogue. While pointing out the huge social changes which none can dispute, he takes a side-swipe at the humorists who between the wars made literary capital out of the village cricket scene. He indicts them for being class-ridden, patronising to 'yokels', stuck in a time-warp of false nostalgia for a world that has long since disappeared, if indeed it ever existed. Supporting his argument is John Arlott, no less, who cites Macdonell's *England Their England* as a prime example of the trend. Now this comes as a surprise to those who have been reading these pages. Firstly, Jack Squire himself never patronised the yokels. He treated them only with civility and generosity. That was the nature of the man; and he didn't much care for Macdonell's account, where he felt <u>he</u> was the one being patronised and misrepresented, not the Blacksmith who could surely look after himself.

As for Sir Derek questioning the scenery?

The oaks and poplars shading a sun-lit green, thatched

cottages ... an old church ... an inn or its sign-board ... long since disappeared under the busy roads, semi-detached houses and television aerials of commuter-land, supermarket society.

Despite the forebodings of the previous chapter, we can find most villages hanging in there, as often as not with cricket being played on a summer's day. Who of us passing in train or car, doesn't take time out to watch the next ball bowled, its fate in the balance, as it's blocked, missed or despatched by total strangers – and share with them, in that fleeting glance, the glorious dream?
... And the dream lives on.